HISTORIC
MAHONE BAY

BRIAN TENNYSON & WILMA STEWART-WHITE

NIMBUS
PUBLISHING

Nimbus Publishing Limited
PO Box 9166
Halifax, NS   B3K 5M8
(902) 455-4286

Printed and bound in Canada

Interior Design: Kathy Kaulbach, Touchstone Design
Cover Design: Heather Bryan
Front cover: *Leo*, a brigantine built by Titus Langille in 1882. See page 37

Library and Archives Canada Cataloguing in Publication

Tennyson, B. D.
Historic Mahone Bay / Brian Tennyson and Wilma Stewart-White.
(Images of our past)
Includes bibliographical references and index.
ISBN 1-55109-558-0

1. Mahone Bay (N.S.)—History. 2. Mahone Bay (N.S.)—Biography.
I. Stewart White, Wilma II. Title. III. Series.

FC2349.M317T45 2006   971.6'23   C2006-901498-1

Canadä   The Canada Council | Le Conseil des Arts
          for the Arts | du Canada

We acknowledge the financial support of the Government of Canada through the Book Publishing Industry Development Program (BPIDP) and the Canada Council, and of the Province of Nova Scotia through the Department of Tourism, Culture and Heritage for our publishing activities.

Dedicated to
Sandy and David,
who supported yet another project.

Preface

It is curious that although Nova Scotia's South Shore has a rich, colourful, and important history, little has been written about it beyond the endless stream of books on privateers and Oak Island treasure. What little has been written tends to focus on the town of Lunenburg, at the expense of other significant communities in the area. Thus, Mather Byles DesBrisay's classic *History of the County of Lunenburg* (1895) allots only a few pages to Mahone Bay, and Winthrop Pickard Bell's magisterial volume, *The "Foreign Protestants" and the Settlement of Nova Scotia* (1961), which chronicles the founding of Lunenburg Township in extraordinary detail, hardly mentions it at all. There is, in fact, no book of any kind devoted exclusively to the town of Mahone Bay, although the Settlers Museum did publish a very interesting and attractive collection of historical photographs in 2004.

Clearly, there was a task to be undertaken, and while we do not claim that *Historic Mahone Bay* presents anything approaching a complete history of the town, we do hope that it is a useful beginning on which others may build. By combining images, history, and anecdotes about the people who have lived in Mahone Bay over the past 250 years, we have attempted to make the book as appealing as possible to a wide readership.

The writing of this book has been a labour of love. One of us has spent many years living in Mahone Bay and has long been active in the preservation of its history and built heritage. The other is new to the area, but, being a historian, was anxious to learn more about his new home. Thus, our partnership combines local knowledge of places and people with the expertise and long experience of a recently retired professional historian. We have enjoyed producing this book and hope that readers will enjoy discovering historic Mahone Bay.

Acknowledgments

I t is far from a truism to say that this book could not have been completed without the cooperation and support of many people and it is a genuine pleasure to be able to thank them here. First and foremost was Joan Foran, who has done so much to sustain the history of Mahone Bay over the years, and who generously shared her knowledge and research notes with us. Others who contributed in various ways include Hedy Armour, Reid Campbell, Isobel Crossland, Ronald Crossland, John Donaldson, Michael Ernst, Martha Farrar, Jenna Hirtle, Victoria Hirtle, Heather Holm, Dorothy Robinson, Scott Robson, Edith Wolter, and Robert Zinck. Sandra Atwell-Tennyson helped in many ways, including proofreading, providing technical assistance, and helping to assemble the final product.

Ralph Getson, curator of the Fisheries Museum of the Atlantic in Lunenburg, not only allowed us to make use of his rich photographic collection but read the chapter on shipbuilding as well. Linda Bedford, curator of the DesBrisay Museum in Bridgewater, and Dan Conlin, curator of the Maritime Museum of the Atlantic in Halifax, gave us full access to the collections of their respective museums and also offered helpful advice and guidance. The staff at the Public Archives of Nova Scotia were, as always, tremendously supportive.

We are especially indebted to those who contributed photographs for use in the book. Their specific contributions are listed elsewhere, but they include Ronald Crossland, Betty Eisenhauer, Joan Foran, David Hennigar, Mertice Hirtle, Evelyn Hutt, Carolyn Kuhn, Bobby Mader, Judith Mader, Richard Rogers, Andrew Whynot, Gary Wilson, J. Franklin Wright, Jean Wright-Popescul, Peter Young, and Terry Young. With regard to the photo credits, the acknowledgment is to those who lent us the pictures, not necessarily to those who took the photographs.

Finally, it is a pleasure to acknowledge the support of Sandra Atwell-Tennyson and David White, who displayed remarkable patience while their spouses spent seemingly endless hours together attempting to unravel the tangled and often obscure history of a little town on the South Shore.

BDT & WS-W
September 10, 2005

Contents

Introduction

There is a little town so quaint, where the ocean breezes blow
Nestled in amongst the hills, where the Mushamush River flows
One of the oldest towns around, where our ancestors came
The sloops they used to sail back then gave this old town its name.

R. E. Joudrey, 2001

The South Shore of Nova Scotia, stretching from Halifax down to Shelburne and beyond, is a series of inlets and bays. Mahone Bay, some eighty kilometres from Halifax, stretches from the Aspotogan Peninsula to Lunenburg and is sheltered from the open ocean by more than three hundred islands and rock outcroppings, the best known being Great Tancook Island and Oak Island. The town of Mahone Bay is situated at the western end of the bay, where two rivers, the Mushamush and the Anney—some local people call it the Anney Anney, others the Little Anney or Ernst Brook, and a few even call it, for reasons unknown, the Maggie Maggie—empty into it. Founded in 1754, Mahone Bay is one of the oldest settlements in Nova Scotia and has achieved international recognition as one of the prettiest towns in Canada, instantly recognizable by its three elegant churches standing side by side along the water's edge.

Although the modern town was only founded in the middle of the eighteenth century, its site was well known to the Mi'kmaq, who called it Mushamush. The Mi'kmaq had a summer camp at Mahone Bay, and it has also been claimed that they held annual powwows at Indian Point, where a burial ground has been identified. The precise location of the Mi'kmaw settlement at Mushamush cannot be determined with certainty, but there is reason to believe there were two sites, one at Indian Point and the other on the hill between Blockhouse and Mahone Bay, near the present town reservoir.

Merligueche, as Lunenburg was known to the Mi'kmaq, was one of the earliest French settlements in Acadie, and Nicolas Denys carried on lumbering operations there from 1632 to 1635. A small fishery developed there as well, and by the late 1740s it was a trading port occupied by twelve to twenty families. There are no references to settlements at Mahone Bay although there was a small French settlement at Mader's Cove, where a mill was erected on the small stream running into the bay.

The origin of Mahone Bay's name has been the subject of considerable speculation. On some early French maps the bay is referred to as La Baye de Toutes Iles or Bay of Many Islands, but the modern name first appears in a coastal survey made in 1736 by the British navigator Thomas Durell, and Jacques Bellin's 1757 map shows Baye Mohone. There seems to be general agreement that *mahonne* is a French word, allegedly derived from a similar Turkish word meaning a low, sleek pirate vessel powered by long oars or sweeps, that was common in the Mediterranean Sea. This name allegedly was applied to the bay because it was frequented by pirates who used such vessels. Over time the word became anglicized and was applied to the village as well.

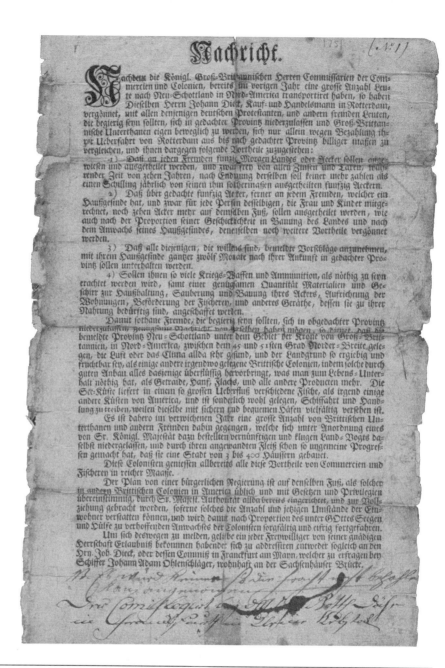

EMIGRATION HANDBILL, C.1750

Whether or not there were many pirates in the area, there was certainly a good deal of rivalry between the English and French along the Atlantic seaboard, which included raiding each other's shipping during the seventeenth and eighteenth centuries. This conflict continued even after the British took possession of mainland Nova Scotia in 1713. The Mi'kmaq, who were allied with the French because of their fear of large-scale British settlement in the region, were also swept up in the conflict. In 1749 the British founded Halifax to offset the threat posed to New England by Fortress Louisbourg in Cape Breton.

The British government was also concerned about the fact that Nova Scotia's population was overwhelmingly French-speaking and Catholic. It therefore decided to encourage English-speaking Protestant settlement in the province by offering land, arms, utensils, and a year's rations. Although the response was overwhelming, most of those who signed up were poor people from London rather than the more desirable farmers or discharged military personnel.

These early settlers, perhaps unsurprisingly, were not generally a great success, and Governor Cornwallis was soon appealing to the Board of Trade to send out more suitable settlers. While this seemed desirable in principle, the predominant mercantile thinking of the day discouraged emigration on the grounds that it constituted a loss of human resources to the nation. From this dilemma arose the idea of recruiting "foreign" Protestants in Europe. It was not a new or especially novel idea. German Protestants had been immigrating to the American colonies, particularly Pennsylvania, since 1683, and the Germans and Swiss among the settlers who founded Halifax had impressed Cornwallis as being "regular, honest and industrious men [who are] easily governed and work heartily."

And so the recruitment campaign was undertaken with the result that 2,724 "foreign Protestants" arrived at Halifax between 1750 and 1752. Recruited primarily from the Palatinate, Wurttemberg, and Hess-Darmstadt in Germany, Montbéliard in France, and Switzerland, most were German speakers although about three dozen families—chiefly those from Montbéliard—had French names and spoke French. About half of the men were farmers or husbandmen and a quarter were tradesmen.

The so-called foreign Protestants were initially kept at Halifax because the hostility of the Mi'kmaq made it unsafe for settlers to venture beyond the palisades, their labour was needed to help with the construction of defensive works, and they had indentured themselves to repay the cost of their transportation. They soon became a problem, however, because they were housed in crowded barracks on the outskirts of the little town, and, not being able to support themselves, they became a financial burden. They also became increasingly frustrated and troublesome.

In the spring of 1753 Governor Peregrine Hopson decided to settle them at Merligueche. Its snug harbour and good surrounding agricultural land were important points, but another consideration was the fact that it was situated on a narrow peninsula that could be fenced off for protection from the Mi'kmaq. Another advantage was that it was not far from Halifax and could potentially provide the garrison town with foodstuffs and cordwood. Hopson therefore ordered a survey of lands at Merligueche, which was now renamed Lunenburg. The prospective settlers met in St. Paul's Church in Halifax and, using playing cards, drew lots for their town grants. Thirty-acre farm lots would be assigned later. Blockhouses, materials and frames for magazines, storehouses and habitations for the people were collected, and ships were engaged at Boston to transport the settlers and their supplies to Merligueche.

The first summer and autumn were spent building houses and clearing land. The surveying of the farm lots was completed in the summer of 1754, when the settlers then began clearing land to start their farms. Thus, Mahone Bay began as an agricultural extension of Lunenburg and for many years it tended to be overshadowed by its larger neighbour.

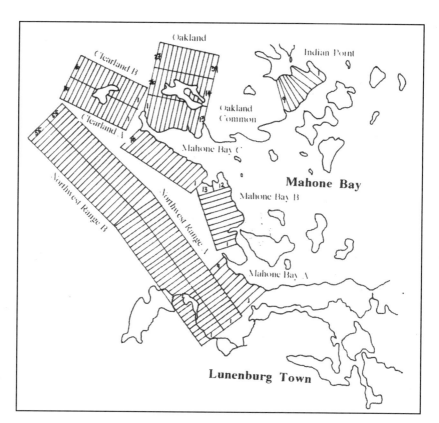

Oakland

Clearland B

Clearland A

Northwest Range B

Northwest Range A

Oakland Common

Mahone Bay C

Indian Point

Mahone Bay B

Mahone Bay

Mahone Bay A

Lunenburg Town

THIRTY-ACRE FARM LOTS, MAHONE BAY, 1754

Meanwhile, the government was anxious to settle some English-speaking people among the foreign Protestants. The government therefore devoted a good deal of attention through 1754 and 1755 to the tentative projects of two separate companies of entrepreneurs that were considering establishing fishing bases in the area. Nothing came of either project, however, apparently because the government thought the entrepreneurs' demands for land grants and free rations for settlers were excessive.

Many claim that Ephraim Cook was the founder of Mahone Bay. Cook was born at Wallingford, Connecticut, in 1699 and was descended from Mayflower founders of Massachusetts. He became a sea captain and commanded *Baltimore*, one of the transports in the Cornwallis expedition that founded Halifax in 1749. He settled there himself and was a prominent merchant and shipowner, as well as a justice of the peace and judge of the Inferior Court of Common Pleas. He was also, as Lunenburg historian Winthrop Pickard Bell observed, a "troublesome" and "cantankerous character" who was soon involved in a number of highly controversial disputes that led to legal actions. Cook then petitioned Charles Lawrence, the new governor of Nova Scotia, in April 1754 for a grant of land at Mahone Bay, where he proposed to build a sawmill and shipyard. He promised to build two vessels, a ship of 160 tons and a schooner of seventy tons, thereby giving employment to many people, and proposed to bring twenty head of breeding cattle from New England, to develop extensive hayfields, and to plant "a great stock of vegetables." He also promised to erect a blockhouse to protect his establishment.

Lawrence agreed to Cook's proposals, apparently because, as he explained to Patrick Sutherland, the officer in charge at Lunenburg, "nothing can contribute more to the advancement and welfare of the Settlement and at the same time to the particular interest of every individual than having Merchants amongst them who have money to spend and a spirit to part with it." Sutherland was therefore instructed to assign a small detachment of his rangers to garrison Cook's blockhouse.

Cook is a rather controversial figure in Mahone Bay's history, perhaps because he did not remain there very long, but also no doubt because he continued to be as cantakerous and troublesome as ever. He began squabbling with Sutherland almost immediately after his arrival and was soon making charges against Joseph Pernette, the lieutenant in charge of the Lunenburg rangers.

When all of Cook's property in Nova Scotia was seized in the spring of 1795 under a court order issued against him in London, he left Mahone Bay and returned to Boston. He eventually returned to Wallingford, where he died in 1774. He is, incidentally, sometimes confused with the Ephraim Cook (1737–1821) who was one of the founders of Yarmouth in the 1760s. They were in fact different people, although they were cousins.

Because most of the early settlers at Mahone Bay were farmers, the community was obviously a rural one, not a town. Cook's sawmill at the mouth of the Mushamush River was one of five in existence "among the out lots" by October 1754, according to Lawrence. These mills provided employment not only for those who worked there, but also for farmers and woodsmen who cut timber to supply them. And at a time when roads were either non-existent or virtually impassable for much of the year, people settled by the water for ease of transportation. Thus, the early development of the town took place in the area lying between the Mushamush and Anney Rivers, which was also where the road from LaHave passed through the Centre Range down to the shore.

Conditions were primitive and hard for the settlers in the early years. Bad weather conditions killed crops and livestock and slowed the development of the village. At the same time, Mi'kmaw raids continued to be a serious problem until the fall of Quebec in 1759 brought about the end of the Anglo-French war and French support of the Mi'kmaq.

The year 1759 was a turning point in other ways as well. The previous year had been very discouraging, quite apart from the Mi'kmaw raids. A forest fire had swept through part of "the country lots" in June 1758, consuming several houses and scorching fields, leaving a number of settlers destitute. It was followed by a disastrous drought, then by a winter that destroyed the root crops, leaving the settlers, in Governor Lawrence's words, "unspeakably…damped and discouraged." The 1759 crops were good, however, and Lawrence reported that "a prodigious quantity of Grain was raised almost equal to their bread, and sufficiency of roots to supply the fleet, the Army and the Inhabitants of Halifax."

Thus, by late 1759 the Lunenburg–Mahone Bay communities had turned the corner. The hostility of the Mi'kmaq had come to an end, and agricultural production was finally reaching the point where the settlers not only were able to feed themselves but could ship their surpluses to Halifax. The area had also become a major source of cordwood for Halifax, to the point that during the recent war one of the colony's armed vessels had been used to escort the "wood vessels" in convoys between Lunenburg, Mahone Bay, and Halifax.

A further indication of the progress being made was the grant of one hundred thousand acres of land to Timothy Houghton of Massachusetts, who proposed to found a settlement at nearby Shoreham (now Chester), also on Mahone Bay. This grant signalled the government's intention to fill the area west of Halifax with reliable, hard-working New England Planters. Houghton arrived from Boston with his wife and three children on August 4, 1759, accompanied by twenty-one settlers.

Another sign of progress was the Board of Trade's decision that Nova Scotia must have an elected representative assembly. It was the only British colony in North America without one, and the board believed that this worked against its goal of attracting settlers from New England. Accordingly, elections were ordered to take place on July 31, 1758, for the first assembly, which would have twenty-two members: four from Halifax and two from Lunenburg Township, plus sixteen members to be chosen at large.

There was a problem at Lunenburg, however, because most of the more than four hundred adult males living there were ineligible to vote, as they had not yet lived seven years in the colony, a requirement for naturalization. On

ASSAULT ON LUNENBURG, 1782

July 5, 1758, Sebastian Zouberbuhler held a special court to administer the oath of allegiance to those settlers who did meet the residency requirement, and Rev. J. B. Moreau "administered the Holy Sacrament to sixty Men, besides Women in the German language." Others were processed as well, such as French-speaking Swiss and a few English-speaking Dutch settlers. Although between eighty and ninety men were now eligible to vote, only fifty-eight of them did so.

Seven candidates—John Creighton, Joshua Mauger, Alexander Kedy, Philip Knaut, Sebastian Zouberbuhler, Leonard Christopher Rudolf, and Paul Anschutz—stood for election. Voting was done publicly, not by secret ballot, and each elector was allowed to vote for two candidates since two members were being elected. Thus, tabulating the results was a complicated process, but in the end Kedy and Knaut were victorious. Kedy was a British immigrant with extensive landholdings and a sawmill at Lilydale, and Knaut was a Lunenburg merchant.

M ahone Bay grew very slowly in the early years. It was completely passed over by the influx of New England Planters in the 1760s, most of whom went to the Annapolis Valley, but land exchanged hands at a remarkable rate for such a small place. This resulted in the consolidation of much land in a few hands, and by 1773 the three biggest landowners in Mahone Bay were Joshua Mauger, Michael Francklin, and Joseph Pernette. They began selling their lands as well, however, and by 1790 George Zwicker and Alexander Kedy had emerged as the largest landowners in the area.

Meanwhile, the American Revolutionary War, which broke out in 1775 and lasted until 1783, had a dramatic impact on Nova Scotia's South Shore communities. There was a good deal of naval and privateering action, and coastal raids were not uncommon. Chester was frequently visited by American privateers, and on July 1, 1782, five or six American privateers, the largest mounting sixteen guns, landed ninety men at Lunenburg, which they proceeded to loot. By the time Major Pernette arrived with troops from LaHave, the Americans were gone. The town had been plundered but was spared from destruction when some of its residents signed a note promising to pay the attackers £1,000 in ransom. The amount of plunder and destruction was estimated at £10,000. Coastal communities in the area continued to be harassed by American privateers, with the result that the militia remained on duty until late October when a detachment of troops arrived at Lunenburg, as well as several armed vessels to patrol the coast.

Anglo-American relations remained tense until 1812, when another war broke out. Again, Nova Scotia's coastal communities were directly affected by the naval war and privateering on both sides. The most dramatic local event was the destruction of the American privateer *Young Teazer* in Mahone Bay on June 26, 1813. *Young Teazer* was spotted off the coast by the Liverpool privateer *Sir John Sherbrooke*, which was patrolling the area accompanied by four smaller vessels, *La Hogue, Orpheus, Castor,* and *Manly. Young Teazer* fled into the bay behind Big Tancook Island, where the wind failed and its pursuers launched boats with a view to boarding and seizing the vessel. DesBrisay says that there was "great excitement" in and around Lunenburg that day and people, fearing that Lunenburg was about to be looted, "were actually employed in carting their

"In Mahon Bay," a sketch by John Elliot Woolford, 1817

belongings out of town." What they didn't know was that one of the officers on *Young Teazer*, Lieutenant Frederick Johnson, was a deserter from the Royal Navy and faced execution if captured. In desperation, he decided that suicide was preferable to hanging and ignited the ship's magazine, destroying the vessel and killing most of the crew as well as himself.

A year later, on the same date, as Will Bird tells the story in *This Is Nova Scotia* (1950), the people of Mahone Bay "were startled to see an apparition sailing into the same water where the *Young Teazer* had been destroyed. As it came nearer they recognized it as the privateer, and then it vanished in a huge puff of flame and smoke. The story spread through the country, and on the next anniversary many were on hand, watching for 'the fire ship.' Sure enough, it appeared again, and it is legend to this day that many persons now living have witnessed the appearance of the ghost ship, and have seen it disappear in flames." Lunenburg journalist W. A. Letson claimed in 1896 that he had "once met an old man who said he was ready to swear he and his sons had seen it." C. H. J. Snider, writing in 1928, went further: "hundreds have seen it; sober-minded, matter-of-fact Nova Scotians who have radio sets in their parlours, cars in their garages, and money in the bank."

In the early nineteenth century, Mahone Bay was still only what historian Ronald McDonald has called "an embryonic village at the head of the bay, nestled below Sugar Loaf Hill," supported by growing agricultural and forestry industries. Foodstuffs, cordwood and lumber were being shipped to Halifax and this led inevitably to the construction of coastal vessels. As *The Times* of Halifax reported in 1840, "every substantial farmer has his coasting shallop, and every

This as-yet uniden-
tified item, which
belonged to Johan
Peter Zwicker Jr.,
(1736–1813) is a fine
example of calligraphy
and illumination.
Zwicker was a lay
preacher who became
known as "Dr."
because he was well
read and had a large
library.

little farmer his few cords of wood, his seventy or eighty bushels of potatoes, his cabbages and eggs, which he sends to the metropolis, and receives in return his supplies of merchandise." Several sketches made by John Elliot Woolford, a British artist who visited in 1817, show a cluster of houses at the head of the bay, and an occasional farmhouse on a cleared thirty-acre lot. Joseph Howe described the village in 1830 as consisting of "snug houses scattered along both sides [of the bay], exhibiting a neatness and a degree of high culture which would put to shame some other parts of the Province I could name."

Even though some British settlers like the Kedys had settled in the area, the population remained overwhelmingly German and continued to speak that language in daily usage for many years. When Lord Dalhousie, the recently appointed lieutenant-governor of Nova Scotia, visited Mahone Bay in 1817 and 1818, he was struck by the fact that the population was still predominantly German and "scarcely do they speak English intelligibly." William Moorsom, writing in 1830, made a similar observation: "The German language is used as frequently as English in the common intercourse of the country people; there are some who hardly ever make use of any other tongue, and the accent is universally foreign, and the pronunciation hard to an English ear."

Meanwhile, there was still a Mi'kmaw settlement on the hill lying between Blockhouse and Mahone Bay in the early years of the nineteenth century, although it gradually disappeared. The Mi'kmaw people suffered terribly during the eighteenth and nineteenth centuries as a result of European immigration to Nova Scotia. The fact that they had sided with the French in the long period of Anglo-French warfare created difficulties in their relationship with the British, and the fact that they were Catholic did not help the situation. The spread of European agricultural settlements gradually forced them onto reserves where they could not pursue their traditional migratory way of life. As well, they were

MI'KMAW FAMILY, c.1910

devastated by the diseases brought by the settlers, to which the Mi'kmaq had not built up a biological resistance, so that by 1861 it was reported that there were only thirty-eight Mi'kmaw people left in Lunenburg County. Happily, the population began to grow again in the second half of the century, and by 1891 there were fifty-nine Mi'kmaq in the county.

The growth of Mahone Bay was reflected in the establishment of the first school about 1815 and the first churches in the 1830s. For the first few years, the school held its classes in people's homes, but on November 1, 1820, a proper school building was opened with William Turner as teacher. Classes were held for only six months of the year, and the teacher was paid quarterly by the parents. In 1861 a new larger school was built nearby, on the shore opposite the future site of the Anglican church. The old schoolhouse became a private residence, but in 1912 it was torn down. Within a decade the new school had also become too small, and the building was sold to Augustus Joudrey, who used it as a blacksmith shop.

By the 1850s Nova Scotia had entered its golden age, when it enjoyed unprecedented prosperity based on its agricultural, forestry, fishing, shipbuilding, and shipping industries. Mahone Bay shared fully in this golden age, as all five industries flourished in and around the village. Forestry and shipbuilding were, of course, obviously interrelated as the town's motto, "Unio Silvae Marisque," which means union of forest and sea, rightly proclaims. The community was, in DesBrisay's words, "a great emporium for cord-wood; and that, besides the lumber furnished by the numerous saw-mills in the surrounding country, forms a chief article of export." There were, by the later part of the nineteenth century, fourteen mills in operation on the Mushamush River. As well, Mahone Bay vessels and men formed a significant component of the so-called Lunenburg fishing fleet.

FIRST SCHOOL, 1820. THE SCHOOL IS THE LITTLE BUILDING BETWEEN THE CHURCHES.

HAYING AT MAHONE BAY, EARLY TWENTIETH CENTURY

CHILDREN GATHERING SEAWEED, EARLY TWENTIETH CENTURY

Shipbuilding soon emerged as the major local industry, aided by the community's excellent location on the western head of a sheltered bay, surrounded by forests and adjacent to rivers capable of providing power for sawmills. The first vessel known to have been built at Mahone Bay was the schooner *Lively*, built in 1804. How many vessels were built at Mahone Bay over the years will probably never be known, although they certainly numbered more than five hundred, not counting the many hundreds of small motorboats and recreational sailboats built in later years.

The first commercial shipbuilder was Elkanah Zwicker, a great-grandson of Peter Zwicker, one of Mahone Bay's original settlers. His first vessel for which we have a record was *Inquisitive*, a one-hundred-ton schooner built in 1848. Other major shipbuilders included John Henry Zwicker, Titus Langille, Jacob Ernst and his sons, Henry Schnare and the Burgoyne brothers, John McLean, and Obed Ham.

The growth of Mahone Bay led some of its citizens to feel that the time had come to give their community an official name. Up to this point the village had been informally known by the name of the bay that it overlooks. A public meeting was held at the Victoria Hall on April 13, 1857, to establish boundaries for the village and to give it a name. Several possibilities were considered, but the majority voted for "Kinburn." Nobody seems to know where this name came from. It has been rather improbably suggested that it came from a Mi'kmaq word meaning "relative or kindred streams" and was therefore appropriate because of the two rivers that empty into the bay at the village site. Others have claimed that it refers to Charles Kinburn, a local military officer in the 1750s of whom there seems to be no trace.

It is more likely that it was inspired by patriotism. The recently concluded Crimean War had included a major naval battle in October 1855 near the Kinburn peninsula, and this resulted in a number of places in Britain and Canada adopting the name. It didn't last long, however, because when the bill was introduced into the Nova Scotia assembly in 1859 to approve the change, seventy-eight men who described themselves as "for the most part being the lineal descendants and some of us now far advanced in life the original settlers ourselves," petitioned against it. Claiming that "the greater number of us are the Bona Fide landed proprietors of Mahone Bay, in Fee Simple," they asserted that the proposed name change had "been got up without our knowledge and consent and in a clandestine manner" by "tenants, boarders and transient persons." The bill was not passed. For several years it became the general practice to refer to the village simply as "Mahone" to distinguish it from the bay, but in time the old name came back into use.

If the 1860s was a period of general prosperity in Mahone Bay and other South Shore communities, it was also a period of political instability. The American Civil War, which broke out in 1861, caused a serious deterioration in Anglo-American relations, and war was feared. There was panic when rumours spread through Nova Scotia in 1864 that a fleet belonging to the Fenians—an Irish nationalist organization active in the United States—had sailed from Maine to attack the province. The militia was called out at Mahone Bay and other coastal communities and ordered "to hold themselves in readiness at a moment's warning." According to tradition, a Fenian warship did indeed sail

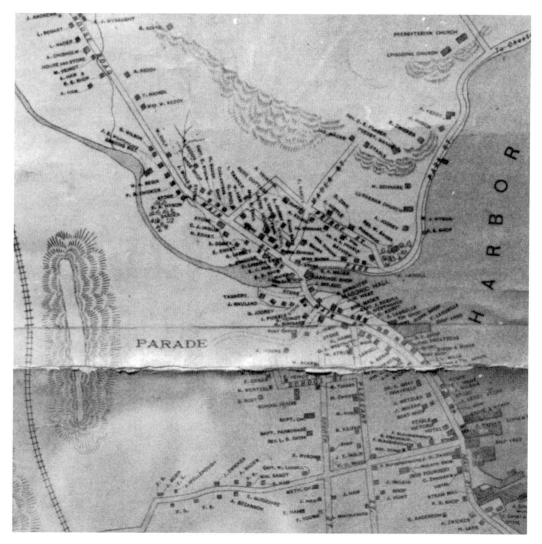

MAHONE BAY,
c.1864–84

Ambrose F. Church was commissioned by the Nova Scotia government in 1864 to create a series of maps, one for each of the province's eighteen counties. Although this map of Mahone Bay is dated 1864, it was not actually completed until the 1880s. Because it cost a dollar to have a house or business included on the map, it cannot be considered accurate.

into Deep Cove at Blandford, across the bay from Mahone Bay, and five Fenian soldiers went ashore for fresh water. A 1934 history of Upper Blandford, written as a school project under the supervision of Ethel Meisner, claims that "while they were there some Indians came out of the woods and cruelly murdered the soldiers" and this explains why the hill by the brook is known as Fenian Hill.

Whether or not this story is true—and it seems improbable as historians know of no Fenian attacks on Nova Scotia—fear of the United States played a significant role in bringing about the confederation of the British North American prov-

ELECTION POSTER, 1886

inces in 1867. This was a highly controversial measure in Nova Scotia, and there was widespread opposition along the South Shore because the area's prosperity was based on international trade, while the proponents of confederation made it quite clear that their ultimate goal was to build a trans-Canadian economy based on industrial development. In the 1867 federal and provincial elections the people of Mahone Bay voted overwhelmingly against the union, and they generally supported repeal candidates for several years afterward.

As was the case with Nova Scotia generally, the period between Confederation and the First World War marked the apex of Mahone Bay's growth and development. From a population of eight hundred in 1871, the vil-

OAKLAND POWER STATION, C.1903

MAHONE BAY ACADEMY, 1914

lage grew to fifteen hundred by 1904. This growth was reflected in the fact that the new school built in 1861 was already too small by 1870, when construction of the first high school began. By 1914 this school was also too small and was replaced by the Mahone Bay Academy, which was built on the same site and remained in use as the town's high school until 1978. Over the years, the Academy produced three Rhodes Scholars: Frank Parker Day, academic, novelist, and commander of the Cape Breton Highlanders in the First World War; William G. Ernst, who entered parliament and served as minister of fisheries in the government of R. B. Bennett; and Denis Stairs, who was for many years a distinguished political scientist at Dalhousie University.

The arrival in 1872 of T. G. Nicol (1852–1931), a Scottish-born entrepreneur, signalled the beginning of a shift in the economic focus of Mahone Bay and, indeed, Nova Scotia generally. Nicol came to build a gang mill for the Kedy brothers. A pioneer in the development of hydroelectric power, he built an electrical generating plant at Clearland that supplied power to Lunenburg. In 1902 Nicol built a generating station at Oakland to provide lighting to Mahone Bay, although there was still no lighting four years later when he sold the company to the village, which also did not proceed as quickly as some thought desirable. *The Signal,* Fred Cox's weekly newspaper, commented acerbically in April 1906 that the village's water commissioners had approved street lighting in February, but "as we are still in total darkness, we take this liberty of reminding our worthy body of the necessity of quick action."

Another indication of the changing nature of the economy came with the completion in October 1889 of the Nova Scotia Central Railway, which linked Mahone Bay to Lunenburg, Bridgewater, and Middleton, where it connected with the Dominion & Atlantic Railway. The Nova Scotia Central was bought out in 1903 by the Halifax & South Western Railway, popularly known as the Hellish Slow & Weary (or Wobbly) Railway, which completed its line linking Mahone Bay to Halifax in 1904. Coupled with a steamship service, which since

MAHONE JUNCTION RAILWAY STATION, 1903

COLLISION AT MAHONE JUNCTION, 1907

the late 1890s had connected Mahone Bay and Lunenburg with Halifax and Yarmouth on a regular schedule, the railway did much to open the area to the nascent tourism industry.

Mahone Bay's first railway station was located on West Main Street, but in 1894 a new and more impressive station was built just behind South Main Street. When the Halifax & South Western Railway took over the Nova Scotia Central Railway in 1903, another new station was built on the northern edge of town at the junction of the railway's main line and the branch line to Lunenburg. For this reason it was called Mahone Junction. People could travel to Halifax, Lunenburg, the Annapolis Valley, Bridgewater, and Yarmouth from Mahone Junction. They also used the train for local travel, such as going into Mahone Bay from Clearland or Blockhouse.

Unfortunately, with the railway came accidents. On October 16, 1905, a train collided with a wagon crossing the tracks at Blockhouse, killing Henry Ernst and his wife and badly injuring his stepson, Arthur Eisenhauer. More serious was the accident that took place at the Mahone Bay station on February 9, 1907, which was one of the worst train accidents in Nova Scotian history. Three men were killed and another injured when an overloaded freight train travelling from Bridgewater went out of control coming down the hill from Blockhouse to Mahone Bay and crashed into a passenger train bound for Middleton. The collision caused the destruction of both engines, four flat cars, and the freight shed, as well as a section of track.

Progress also brought other kinds of problems and concerns. The people of Mahone Bay, despite—or perhaps because of—the community's hard-drinking tradition, voted overwhelmingly in favour of prohibition in the national referendum on the matter in 1894, although the federal government took no action because the overall results were indecisive. And in April 1906 a controversy erupted over the allegedly pernicious influence of pool halls on the community's moral standards. "Some of the good people of Mahone are shocked," an anonymous citizen wrote to the editor of the weekly paper *The Signal*, to discover that Captain Ben Westhaver had acquired a pool table, and he felt obliged to close his facility for several days "until he got advice from his Solicitor as to how he could keep objectionable persons out of his rooms."

Another unidentified letter writer complained, however, that "these good meaning people who are so shocked don't know their ideas are the ancient intellectual fossils of a by-gone age." There were, he claimed, eight pool tables in Bridgewater and "about the same number" in Lunenburg. Indeed, they were even to be found in YMCA facilities, and, to close the argument, even in the "Harbour for retired sea captains on Staten Island." The people of Mahone Bay, he asserted, were "not a pool playing people" but "hardy fishermen, toilers on the deep" who were entitled to some innocent recreation. Besides, "there are notices posted up in the pool room forbidding the use of profane and obscene language and not allowing boys who are supposed to be at school. And persons on the booze are unwelcome visitors." However, W. H. Longley, who was principal of the Mahone Bay school from 1904 to 1906, claimed that Westhaver, with whom he boarded at the American House, was a somewhat disreputable if likeable old scoundrel with a serious drinking problem who was running an illegal saloon in connection with his pool room.

The First World War, which broke out in August 1914, had a major impact on Mahone Bay, as it did on other towns and villages throughout Nova Scotia. Young men rushed to join up, and in 1916 the Lunenburg and Annapolis County militia regiments were combined to form the 219th Battalion. At home, the shipbuilding industry boomed during the war, and the McLean yard acquired the John H. Zwicker shipyard. Although there was considerable German submarine activity in the Atlantic Ocean, and often quite close to shore, the Lunenburg–Mahone Bay fishing fleet escaped any loss until August 1918, when nine vessels were sunk. At the war's conclusion, the village joined in the celebrations organized by Rev. Ned Harris. A highlight of the celebrations was the burning of an effigy of the kaiser made by Harris on Spion Kop Hill.

In 1923 a war memorial was placed at Mahone Bay's main intersection. The citizens of the town paid for it through a campaign led by Harris and a contribution from the Mahone Bay Women's Institute. The monument, which records the names of twenty-three local men killed in the war, was designed by Harris. Curiously, in view of the predominantly German background of Mahone Bay's population, it features a Celtic cross, the official explanation being that it was "the cross of the old Scottish Race so appropriate for our New Scotland and our Nova Scotia Highlanders," a regiment that included many men from the South Shore.

The village was incorporated as a town in 1919, and Arthur Ernst, a member of the shipbuilding family, was elected the first mayor. In May 1921 the Mahone Bay Fire Department was established with nearly thirty volunteers equipped with a chemical-hose truck and a pump mounted on a trailer. The first

UNVEILING THE WAR MEMORIAL, 1923

The unveiling of the war monument on May 24, 1923, took on an unusually festive air because it was combined with the annual Empire Day celebrations. This photograph shows Lieutenant-Governor MacCallum Grant addressing the large crowd at the unveiling ceremony, with Ned Harris at his side.

chief was E. A. Ernst, who served for many years. When Halifax journalist Clara Dennis visited in 1925, she thought it a "wonderful little town." This picture was somewhat deceptive, however. Mahone Bay had in fact reached its peak by the turn of the century, if not earlier, and its population was already beginning to decline.

Agriculture and lumbering, at one time the mainstays of the local economy, were becoming marginal, and even the fishing and shipping industries were encountering difficulties as they struggled against foreign competition and tried to keep pace with technological changes. Moreover, the region's youth were steadily being drained off to New England and central Canada. Mahone Bay also suffered as a result of competition from the larger nearby towns of Lunenburg and Bridgewater. This was, perhaps, reflected in the fact that the exhibition building built in 1885 as a venue for agricultural exhibitions and other events was not a success, nor was the race track built near the railway station in 1895.

Mahone Bay struggled to survive during the 1920s, helped to some extent by the fact that its shipyards continued to be unexpectedly busy. Declining employment in the fishery was being at least partially offset by rum-running, a new enterprise brought about by the introduction of prohibition by both the Canadian and American governments at the end of the war. One cannot help thinking back to Mahone Bay's alleged origins, when pirate boats operated among the many islands. Smuggling liquor provided badly needed revenue to

TOWN HALL, 1920S In 1920 this building was purchased from A. C. Zwicker for use as the town hall. It was located behind the present post office on South Main Street. In 1934 a new town hall was acquired and this building was sold, moved around the corner, and converted into residential housing. The first of the town's bandshells can also be seen.

Lunenburg, Mahone Bay, and other coastal communities, and the men who participated in it were generally otherwise law-abiding fishermen and sailors who saw an opportunity and took advantage of it. It would be highly misleading, however, to conclude that Mahone Bay and other coastal communities enjoyed great prosperity in the 1920s. While some people made money in shipbuilding and rum-running, times were hard for most people.

But if the 1920s were difficult, the 1930s were even worse because of the Great Depression that descended on the entire country. Shipbuilding virtually collapsed while prices for agricultural, fishery, and forestry products plummeted. The town was rescued from the Depression, as indeed was the country, by the outbreak of the Second World War, which ended unemployment and created a huge demand for food, materials, and ships.

Although shipbuilding continued to flourish for a few years after the war, Mahone Bay could not be described in the late 1940s as an especially prosperous community. In 1947–48 it had the highest death rate in the province, the highest rate of tuberculosis, and the third lowest birth rate. Meanwhile, its liquor store reported the highest per capita sales in the province in 1949, a level twice that of nearby Lunenburg. William Hirtle, a local educator, claimed in 1950 that "many people with real ambition and ability have been leaving the town," which had developed a "defeatist attitude." When shipbuilding largely collapsed in the 1960s, leaving only a few small boatbuilders in the area, an era came to an end.

Clearly, the town had to reposition itself, and the obvious—and perhaps only—alternative to shipbuilding was tourism. Chester had long been a popular

**ABERDEEN HOTEL,
1907**

In 1934 the Aberdeen Hotel on West Main Street, which had been built in 1848, was purchased from Austin Spidle for use as the new town hall. This photograph, taken in 1907, shows the building after the front tower was added. Its appearance has not changed much since then, except that the balconies have been removed.

spot for summer visitors, especially from the United States, and Lunenburg, which was suffering the same socioeconomic problems as Mahone Bay, was already making the transition to a tourist economy. Mahone Bay had at least as much potential as Lunenburg because of its magnificent physical location and rich architectural heritage. It was, as the writer A. J. McDougald had observed as long ago as 1888, "pleasantly nestled at the head of a bay, which in grandeur of scenery, facilities for bathing and fishing, defies competition."

Halifax journalist J. A. Bell had predicted in 1870 that Mahone Bay would become "a favourite and, perhaps, fashionable place of resort" when the railways were completed. It took longer than that, but modern transportation systems and unprecedented prosperity in Canada, perhaps especially in the Halifax area, have combined with effective local leadership to make Mahone Bay a tourism destination. Described by some as the prettiest village in Canada, since the 1980s it has become a major destination for visitors not only from neighbouring communities but from all over the world. Its picturesque scenery and wonderful eighteenth- and nineteenth-century homes have also attracted seasonal and permanent settlers, who are contributing to its rebirth.

Chapter 1

The Islands

**SHEEP ISLAND (RIGHT), WITH ANDREWS ISLAND IN BACKGROUND,
AS SEEN FROM GIFFORD ISLAND, LOOKING TOWARDS THE TOWN OF MAHONE BAY**

Mahone Bay—that is, the bay itself—is 285 square kilometres in size and is celebrated for its large number of islands. Locals like to claim that there are 365 of them, one for each day of the year. Joseph Howe, on the other hand, observed in 1830, that "there must be a couple of hundreds," and David Stevens, the well-known boatbuilder who spent a lifetime sailing on the bay, claimed that he had counted no more than a hundred. The truth really depends on how one defines an "island." If all the rock outcroppings known as the Racketts are included, the total does perhaps exceed three hundred. Whatever the precise number, however, Howe was undoubtedly right when he observed that "they make up a grand and beautiful panorama, which changes and moves as you ride along. Many times you think you are looking at some peninsula striking away from the main[land], until on a nearer approach you find it surrounded by water."

The islands are more than scenic, however; they played an important part in the history of the area, and they continue to play a large role in defining its character. They also help to shelter the community from the open sea. In the early years they provided safe and secluded anchorages for pirates and privateers, and some were the sites of bloody attacks by Mi'kmaw raiders. Some islands were occupied very soon after the arrival of the European settlers, whereas others were only occupied much later by people attracted by the romance of living—at least in the summer months—on an island. Some remain unoccupied to this day, and the Mahone Islands Conservation Association is presently attempting to purchase some of them so that they can be protected from development and preserved for general public use.

Cross Island, which lies near the entrance to Lunenburg harbour, possesses one of the finest harbours on Nova Scotia's South Shore: narrow but deep and sheltered. It also has the oldest lighthouse in Lunenburg County, built in 1832. As the island was owned and occupied by Jacob Smith at the time, he became the first keeper of the light. He was paid £100 per year, plus £15 as a fuel allowance. Unfortunately, the original historic lighthouse was destroyed by fire in 1960. Because of its fine harbour, there was a prosperous fishing community on Cross Island for many years, as well as a lobster cannery. In the early twentieth century there were sixteen families, and the island had its own school. But as fish became scarce, boats were sold and people moved to the mainland. Today the only occupants of the island are a half dozen families who maintain cottages there.

Heckman's Island, situated at the southern side of the bay directly east of Lunenburg, is named after the Heckman family, which settled there prior to 1830. Before that it was known as Creighton's Island, because it was part of the lands granted to John Creighton, the Halifax merchant who settled in Lunenburg. It then became Hebb's Island because Adam Hebb acquired land there in 1775. His son, also called Adam, was still living there in the 1840s. About 125 people lived there in 1871. Today, having been joined to the mainland by a causeway, Heckman's Island is a popular summer resort community. Nearby Quaker Island marks the western entrance to Chester harbour and was so named because a number of Quakers came from New England to establish a whale fishery there. When they were unable to purchase the island, they returned home but the name stuck.

Generally speaking, those islands that were settled were used for fishing and agriculture. Kaulbach Island, for example, which is just off Indian Point, was owned by James Heisler, who had a small farm there in the early twentieth century. He became the first lighthouse keeper in 1914 and served until 1940, when his son Reuben took over, serving until the light was automated in 1960. Clay Island, however, which is close to Quaker Island, was so named because it provided "superior material for brick-making," according to DesBrisay, while Mason's Island supplied builders at Halifax and other places "with sand of good quality. Thousands of bushels of gravel are obtained for garden walks in the city, and some of it is used in the public gardens there."

The decline of the salt fishery and its replacement by the fresh-fish trade, as well as the introduction of motorized boats, made it increasingly unnecessary for fishermen to live on the islands, with the result that permanent settlements on them have generally declined in the last half century. Those who remain have been joined by seasonal residents, however, and the beauty of the islands remains undiminished.

NORTHWEST COVE, TANCOOK, C.1900

The largest and most populated of the islands is Big Tancook, which is about seven miles from Chester. The Mi'kmaq called it Uktankook, meaning the place facing the open sea. In the 1750s it was known as Tencook and in 1761 it was officially named Queen Charlotte Island, at the same time that the bay was named Charlotte Bay. As we know, neither name stuck. Tancook Island was granted to Captain Patrick Sutherland, who commanded the troops at Lunenburg, but it subsequently reverted to the Crown. In the 1780s it was surveyed, and in 1792 it was divided into two portions that were granted to John Henry Flieger, described as a gentleman of Halifax, and George Grant, a Halifax merchant.

The author George Bellerose has described Tancook as looking from the mainland "like a skipped stone about to sink beneath the sea." The reference to a stone is more than apt because, as he says, "despite its summer greenery, much of the island is little more than a rock disguised by a thin layer of rocky soil." Nonetheless, the original settlers were farmers, and by 1829, according to T. C. Haliburton, there were thirty families on the island. By the turn of the century there were some 500 people there, but despite the introduction of a ferry service in 1935 and a cable bringing electricity in 1952, the population subsequently declined, and today only about 190 people live there. Many others spend their summers there, no doubt because, as the writer Harry Bruce has observed, "whether fog enshrouds Big Tancook or the sun shines on it from a clear blue sky, it is simply beautiful."

NANCY, **1920s**
Tancook Island soon became the home of respected shipbuilders as well. The first vessel known to have been built there was *Nelson,* a forty-ton schooner built in 1818, whose builder remains unknown. Many more followed. Some of the best-known and most productive boatbuilders were Reuben Heisler, who built at least thirty-five vessels; Stan Mason, who built at least fifty-three; Alvin Stevens, who built twenty; and Amos Stevens, who built forty-six vessels. Other important builders were the Langilles—Alfred, Joshua, Vernon, and David—and Warren Pearl. The Tancook builders even developed their own unique vessel, the Tancook Whaler. It was a modified schooner with both ends pointed, capable of being sailed or rowed, and light enough to haul up onto the beach when not in use. The first Tancook Whaler is said to have been built by Alfred Langille about 1880.

The *Lunenburg Progress-Enterprise* reported in June 1894 that "a whaler built by Mr. Amos Stevens, of Tancook, was recently bought by the officers of the Royal Engineers, Halifax, for the sum of $300. She will become a member of the Nova Scotia yacht squadron. Last year Mr. Stevens sold one to the officers of the Royal Artillery. She sailed a number of races last summer, several of which she won. She has sailed but one race so far this season, coming in an excellent third." The last boatyard on Tancook Island was that of Stan Mason, who retired in 1948 and turned the business over to his son, David. Stan later moved to Chester, where he and another son, Leslie, established S. G. Mason & Son, a company that packaged vegetables, fruit, sauerkraut, and garden produce. In 1982 Howard and Sam Rodenhiser built the last vessel at the former Mason boatyard, and the building was subsequently demolished. This photo shows the Tancook whaler *Nancy* anchored at Peggy's Cove in the 1920s.

TRAP-FISHING OFF TANCOOK, C.1974
It wasn't long before the men of Tancook Island became major players in the fishing industry. This wonderful photograph shows Douglas Young (front) and his cousin Gerald Baker trap-fishing mackerel off Tancook Island.

MAKING SAUERKRAUT, 1970s

Tancook Island is best known for its sauerkraut, which is produced from the island's main agricultural crop, cabbages. Islanders take great pride in the quality of their sauerkraut, a South Shore delicacy reflecting the area's strong German heritage. Mainland producers often try to improve their sales by claiming that their product is genuine "Tancook-style" sauerkraut. The late Calvin Hutt, once called "the king of sauerkraut," is shown here processing his cabbage to make the famous Tancook sauerkraut.

Oak Island, Chester Bay, where Capt. Kidd buried his Gold

**OAK ISLAND,
c.1910**

Oak Island is undoubtedly the best known of the islands. One of the smaller
ones, it is very close to the mainland and is in fact now connected to it by a
causeway. It was included in the crown grant of one hundred thousand acres
made to the original settlers of Chester in 1759. The cartographer J. F. W.
DesBarres named it Gloucester Island in 1773, but sometime before 1790 it
became known as Oak Island, apparently because it was the only island in the
bay that was covered in red oak trees. It was first surveyed and divided into
lots by William Nelson in 1785, but John McMullen and Daniel McInnis are
thought to have been the first settlers there. Another early resident was Samuel
Ball, a former slave from South Carolina who, with his wife Mary, worked a
thirty-six-acre farm on Oak Island until his death in 1845.

Mahone Bay was famous for being the haunt of pirates in the seventeenth
century. The idea that there might be buried treasure on one of the islands originated, according to DesBrisay, when an old man in New England claimed on his
deathbed that he had served with Captain William Kidd and "had many years
previously assisted that noted pirate and his followers in burying over two mil-
lions of money beneath the soil of a secluded island east of Boston." The search
began, focusing on Oak Island, in the summer of 1795, after sixteen-year-old
Daniel McInnis Jr. discovered ring bolts in rocks, moss-covered stumps, over-
grown pathways, and a tackle-block hanging from the limb of an old oak tree in
a clearing. He and two friends dug a hole sixty centimetres deep and struck a tier
of flagstones. Removing these stones, they discovered a deeper pit. Three metres
down they encountered a tier of oak logs, which they also removed. They then
dug another five and a half metres. At this point they gave up, but others carried
on where they left off. Excavations continued throughout the nineteenth and
twentieth centuries, involving increasingly heavier equipment and larger amounts

of capital, giving a double meaning to the term "money pit." Historian Mark Finnan, author of the most recent book on the subject, concludes that Oak Island is "a major archeological/historical site, but we may never find out…what its significance is to Nova Scotia, Canada and maybe the world." This photograph shows Oak Island from the mainland before the causeway was built.

Oak Island is not the only island on which pirates are thought to have buried their treasure. According to DesBrisay, a pirate treasure was actually discovered on Hobson's Nose in 1830, and Plum Island was for many years searched by various expeditions equipped with old plans and charts in search of a treasure allegedly buried there by Captain Edward Swede, a pirate who frequented the area about 1669. Clay Island and Redmond's Island have also been the scenes of much digging and trenching, and Spanish silver coins have been found on Graves's Island.

EAST IRONBOUND ISLAND, 1909

One of the more isolated islands is East Ironbound Island, which was known until the 1940s as Chester Ironbound Island to distinguish it from West Ironbound Island, at the mouth of the LaHave River. It is 2.4 kilometres south of the Aspotogan Peninsula and received its name because of its iron-gray stone. There was a fishing community on the island for many years, which Frank Parker Day immortalized in his 1927 novel *Rockbound*, a gritty tale of the hard lives endured by fishermen and their families. Because there is no protected harbour on Ironbound, most of the fishermen used oxen to haul their boats onshore. Before a school was built on the island, its children went to the little school on Big Tancook, six kilometres away by boat. Although there were about forty people still living there in the 1960s, most have since moved to the mainland.

The original lighthouse was built in 1867, but it burned down and was replaced in 1871. It is considered a rare example of mid-nineteenth century lighthouse design. Indeed, lighthouse historian Rip Irwin describes it as "one of a kind and best exemplifies the lifestyle of the folks who kept our lighthouses in a bygone era." The first keeper was Edward Young, but four generations of the Finck family kept the lighthouse over a sixty-year period, and when Violet Finck celebrated her 108th birthday in January 2002, she was undoubtedly the oldest lighthouse keeper in Canada. This photograph shows some visitors to East Ironbound Island in 1909 and perhaps helps to explain why Day entitled his book *Rockbound*.

HOBSON'S NOSE LIGHTHOUSE, 1937 Many islands were so small that they remained unoccupied except for lighthouse keepers and their families. Some, like Hobson's Nose, have virtually disappeared because of erosion, leaving only an automated light on an outcropping of rock. This photograph shows the lighthouse on Hobson's Nose Island in 1937, with lobster traps stacked on staging on the beach.

Westhavers Light, Mahone Bay Harbour, Mahone, N. S.

WESTHAVER ISLAND

Lighthouses were needed, of course, because the waters along the South Shore, and especially in the entrance to Mahone Bay, are treacherous. There were many shipwrecks over the years, such as that of *Flo F. Mader*, a schooner built by J. H. Zwicker in 1896, which ran aground on Westhaver Island in January 1923. Efforts by the coast guard cutter *Acadia* to refloat it proved fruitless and the wreckage remains. According to Michael Ernst, the harbour froze over during the following winter and skating parties took place at the site, which included building fires on the ship's decks! The lighthouse, built in 1882, was automated following the Second World War.

Because it provides a nesting habitat that is critical to the survival of the endangered roseate tern and is important to migratory songbirds, Westhaver Island has been designated an Important Bird Area by Bird Life International, the Canadian Nature Federation, and Bird Studies Canada. No hunting or trapping is allowed there, and during the nesting period of April to mid-August visitors must acquire a permit.

MASCOTTE, C.1930   W. A. Letson wrote in 1896 that "on a fine night" one could see from the balcony of the lighthouse on Green Island "seven other coast lights beckoning to safety the homeward bound." While lighthouses are pretty and project a romantic image, their keepers lived lonely and sometimes hazardous lives. When DesBrisay visited Green Island in 1876, the keeper, Walter Pearl told him that he was his first visitor in two years, other than the government vessel that brought out supplies annually and "his father and brothers, and fishermen passing occasionally to and from their nets." Indeed, the island was so isolated that a cow that had been taken there, "seeming ill-satisfied with the change thus made in her life...tried to get into a boat leaving for Tancook, and persisted in the attempt till beaten back by the waves." There were occasions when the lighthouse keeper on Green Island actually ran out of food and water. In April 1882 Walter Pearl and his youngest son, Benjamin, disappeared while sailing to Mason's Island.

The name of Green Island was changed in 1914 to Pearl Island, in order to distinguish it from other islands of the same name in the area. Fittingly, the new name honoured the Pearl family, which provided four generations of lighthouse keepers there. Because of the isolation and deteriorating condition of the keeper's house, Albert Pearl's family eventually refused to live any longer on the island, so he remained there alone until January 1962, when he mysteriously disappeared. Presumably he had fallen into the water but his body was never found. The Pearl Island lighthouse was subsequently automated so nobody has lived on the island since 1962, but, according to Rip Irwin, "some people say the ghost of Albert Pearl still occupies the island, especially on dark and stormy nights."

Like Westhaver Island, Pearl Island has been designated an Important Bird Area by Bird Life International, the Canadian Nature Federation, and Bird Studies Canada. There was a proposal in 1998 to build a memorial on the island to the victims of Swissair Flight 111, which had crashed just offshore in September of that year. Sharp protests from environmental groups, as well as the fact that the island is isolated and difficult to access, resulted in the decision to build two memorials on the mainland instead.

Communication between coastal communities and the islands was maintained by coastal freighters and later by ferries. *Kinburn* was built by the Ernst shipyard in 1917 and used by the company to connect Mahone Bay with Halifax, stopping at Chester and Big Tancook Island. Built at Dartmouth in 1896 for the Acadia Sugar Refinery, *Mascotte* was used in 1902 as a summer ferry between Mahone Bay and Chester, typically carrying as many as a hundred passengers. From 1902 until 1934 Captain George Naas operated it between Lunenburg, Bayport, Cross Island, and Corkum's Island. Regular year-round ferry service between Chester and Tancook finally began in 1935 after two women, Mrs. Leander Cross and Mrs. Herbie Young, fell ill and died as a result of not being moved quickly to a mainland hospital.

Willis Crooks operated the first ferry, using his two-masted schooner, *Gerald L. C.*, which was at that time the largest boat on the island. For many years the round-trip fare was 25¢ for passengers, 10¢ per hundredweight for freight, $1 per thousand feet of lumber, and $1 per ton of coal. The government-operated ferry in use since 1964 is *William G. Ernst*, named after the Mahone Bay lawyer and politician who briefly served as minister of fisheries in the R. B. Bennett government in 1935 and was instrumental in establishing the ferry service. It has been claimed that Ernst had his car, a Model T, carried to Tancook by two dories so that he could campaign on the island during one of his election campaigns, and this may have helped to persuade him of the need for a ferry.

Chapter 2

Shipbuilding

ERNST SHIPYARD, C.1900

Although Mahone Bay began shipbuilding early in its history and soon became one of the most important sites in the province, its contribution to the industry and to the so-called Lunenburg fishing fleet has tended to be overlooked or underrated. Indeed, accounts of these industries not only focus on Lunenburg, they tend to include information from Mahone Bay as though the two communities were one. And yet Mahone Bay shipbuilders are known to have built at least five hundred vessels and very likely more than that, compared to the approximately nine hundred vessels built at Lunenburg.

The first ship known to have been built at Mahone Bay was the schooner *Lively*, built in 1804. Unfortunately, we don't know who built it; nor do we know who built *Mary Ann* (1817) or *Ann* (1824). The first vessel whose builder can be identified was the schooner *James William*, built by Frederick Hiltz in 1841, but by then at least thirty vessels had been built in the village. Because Hiltz's yard at Clearland was a kilometre from the bay, the schooner was loaded onto a sled built for the purpose and dragged by thirty-six yoke of oxen down to the shore to be launched. Several more vessels were built in the 1840s, and by 1850 at least seventy-five had been built at Mahone Bay. In the 1850s and 1860s another seventy-three vessels were built, and the industry continued to thrive through the rest of the century.

For the most part, Mahone Bay's shipbuilders built schooners and other smaller vessels ranging from forty to two hundred tons, which were used for fishing or coastal freighting. As the years passed, however, there was a trend towards larger vessels, which were required for the foreign trade that developed with the United States, the West Indies, and elsewhere. But what records survive suggest that Mahone Bay's shipbuilders did not build many of these large square-rigged vessels that commonly exceeded one thousand tons.

Smaller boat builders in recent years have included Stephen Slaunwhite who, like his grandfather, built schooners and other boats at Mader's Cove from 1976 until his death in 1996; Cecil Heisler, who carries on the business established by his grandfather William at Gifford Island in 1921; John Steele, who designed and built yachts and power boats on Covey Island before moving to Petite-Rivière; and Bill Lutwick, who has been building and repairing boats at Indian Point since 1984.

Little remains to remind the world of how important the shipbuilding industry once was to the development and identity of Mahone Bay. But the town remembers its proud history, with its annual Wooden Boat Festival, during which Mahone Bay's historic waterfront is once again the focus of attention, its proud history is recalled, and the skills of its boatbuilders are displayed for all to admire.

LEO, 1882

The first commercial shipbuilder was Elkanah Zwicker (1820–74), a great-grandson of Peter Zwicker Sr., one of the original settlers of Mahone Bay. His yard was located at the present site of the Save Easy grocery store's parking lot on Main Street. Zwicker built at least twelve vessels, including seven schooners, a barque, and a brigantine. In 1850 he built the first schooner called *Blue Nose*, for Casper and Peter Eisenhaur of Lunenburg. Titus Langille (1832–1892), one of seven sons— five of whom became shipbuilders—of Jean Pierre "Peter" Langille and his wife Mary Elizabeth Eisenhaur, took over Elkanah Zwicker's shipyard in 1862. Over the years he built at least sixty-five vessels including, the brigantine *Prussia* (362 tons, 1890), which his nephew Joshua Langille considered "the finest vessel that ever sailed out of Mahone Bay harbour," and two steamships. Although "a cranky man," according to his nephew, Langille was recognized as a fine craftsman, and DesBrisay asserted that Mahone Bay owed its "superiority in this art [shipbuilding] chiefly to the Langilles and the Zwickers, who may be called self-made men, and who, if they had followed their occupation on wider fields of action, would have won a far larger share of fame." Langille built *Leo*, a brigantine, in 1882.

**SCHNARE'S
SHIPYARD, C.1900**

Henry Schnare's shipyard was located on the waterfront across from the Lutheran and Presbyterian churches. Because the water was shallow there, he was unable to launch his vessels in the usual upright manner. Instead, the spars were put in place and cables were fastened to the tops of the masts in order to pull the vessel into the water on its beam ends. When the tide came in, the ship would float. Shortly after his arrival in Mahone Bay in April 1884, Ned Harris found it necessary to apologize to his mother for not having written to her sooner: "I should have got this letter written last evening after tea but that time was spent in the excitement of watching the first launch [of the season]. One of the shipyards is right opposite the rectory, about 200 yards away, so the front gate was a splendid place to watch it from. The vessel was a good sized schooner, fitted up very nicely, and she looked very pretty sliding off. Of course there was great cheering. Two more are just ready to follow her. These vessels are all for the fleet which goes off fishing to the Banks."

ZWICKER'S SHIPYARD, 1910

Another major shipbuilder was John Henry Zwicker (1833–1913), Elkanah Zwicker's brother, whose yard was located to the left of the present government wharf. His first vessel, built in 1862, was the schooner *Delight*. He built one of Mahone Bay's most celebrated ships, *Kinburn*, in 1873. A twelve-hundred-ton full-rigged ship that carried twenty-six sails, it was wrecked in the Gulf of St. Lawrence in 1889. It is not clear how many ships Zwicker built, but DesBrisay claimed in 1895 that in addition to *Kinburn* he had built three barquentines, seven brigantines, 132 schooners, and three whalebacks (designed to carry coal for the Little Glace Mining Company). One local historian, Hilda Burgoyne, later claimed that Zwicker built a total of 162 vessels.

MAGGIE BELLE,
1903

This photograph shows the completed *Maggie Belle*, a ninety-nine-ton brigantine built by Zwicker, beside a vessel still under construction, in 1903. *Maggie Belle* was built for Abraham Ernst, and was used to carry salt fish to Puerto Rico and Trinidad. It caught fire on March 13, 1917, and foundered off St. Michael's in the Azores.

JACOB ERNST, c.1890

The Ernst shipyard was founded by Jacob Ernst (1809–1901), a grandson of Christian Ernst. Jacob had a large farm in Blockhouse and began his business career with a general store there. About 1869 he bought land in Mahone Bay and built a store, just in time for his new wharf to be destroyed by the so-called Saxby Gale of October 4–5, 1869, which produced a massive tidal wave. His seventh son, Abraham (1849–1911), carried on this business and soon began shipbuilding as well. He also built about thirty homes in Mahone Bay over the years. Abraham's sons, Selvyn and Willis, ran the company for a number of years, then Willis carried on alone until the Second World War. The shipyard was located at the western end of the village, on a site that is now the parking lot for Reinforced Plastic Systems. Over the years, the shipyard built at least one hundred ships, including vessels designed specifically for the rum-running business in the 1920s.

DRYING FISH, ERNST SHIPYARD, c.1910

The Ernst shipyard was a fully integrated enterprise. In addition to building vessels, it milled, sawed, and planed logs at its own mill. It also operated twelve vessels that fished and hauled timber and other commodities to the West Indies, and it not only cured and packed fish but made the boxes as well. It had a store located at what is now the site of the government wharf, which fitted out fishing and other vessels for their voyages and also did a large trading business in the town and neighbouring districts as well. Fred Mosher recalls enjoying some good times in the main building of the Ernst complex. "On the first floor, northwest corner, was an office. After playing hide and seek in the timber piles of the work yard, Doris Ernst would get a key to that office and a phonograph and we would dance there for a while. It had a good floor for dancing."

ERNST SHIPYARD
WORKERS, 1930S

According to Bobby Mader, whose grandfather Freeman ("Rigger Tom") was a rigger, the Ernst store brought supplies in from Halifax "and then people would go there that worked [at] the shipyards and get their groceries and things and that would be charged against them and at the end of the month when they went to square up sometimes they owed money and they had no money to pay." Freeman Mader was in charge of rigging the original *Bluenose*. Ray Rhuland recalls that his father, who worked as a skilled carpenter at the Ernst yard, "got ten cents an hour, ten hour days. He got one dollar a day. There was nine of us to look after." To put this in perspective, however, Orren Joudrey, who was a clerk in Dr. Pickels's pharmacy in the 1890s, earned forty-three cents a day for a twelve-hour day. On the other hand, Freeman Mader paid his workers between twelve and fifteen cents an hour.

BURGOYNE SHIPYARD, OAKLAND, 1920S

This delightful photograph, taken by Wallace MacAskill in the 1920s, provides a rare glimpse of the Burgoyne shipyard in Oakland. Henry Schnare's shipyard is across the bay in the background. A man can be seen working in the foreground.

JOHN MCLEAN SHIPYARD, 1880S

The McLean shipyard was founded in 1865 by John McLean, although it did not emerge as one of the most important yards in Mahone Bay until later in the century. Allegedly a cousin of Donald McKay—the Massachusetts shipbuilder whose *Flying Cloud* was one of the most famous clipper ships of the nineteenth century—he came to Mahone Bay from Shelburne after having earned his credentials as a master shipbuilder at the age of twenty-one. Like the Ernsts, though on a smaller scale, McLean operated four vessels in the fishing and shipping industries.

McLean shipyard, c.1900
Mahone Bay's shipyards were, for the most part, situated right on South Main Street. As can be seen in this photograph, the bow of this vessel about to be launched from the McLean yard juts out into the street and is right beside the McLean shop. John MacLean is facing the camera in the foreground.

Crofton McLeod, **1901**
This wonderful photograph shows the McLean yard's just-launched eighty-five-ton *Crofton McLeod* sailing on Mahone Bay with John McLean observing it from the shore. The vessel was wrecked on a reef in Canso harbour in May 1908.

JOHN W. MILLER, 1918

John McLean's sons Charles and William eventually joined the company in 1882 and 1897 respectively, and when he died in 1910 they carried on the business. They gave up shipbuilding for a while prior to the outbreak of the First World War and concentrated on operating their fishing fleet and outfitting vessels, but in 1917 they returned to shipbuilding and even took over the Zwicker yard, because of the wartime need for vessels. This photograph shows the tern schooner *John W. Miller* about to be launched in 1918, next to the new shed built in 1917–18 following the purchase of the Zwicker yard. *John W. Miller* was used by J. C. Crosbie Ltd. of St. John's, Newfoundland, in its South American trade. It sank in heavy weather on December 30, 1931, but the crew was rescued by a passing German vessel.

OBED. A. HAM
Marine Architect

YACHT, SHIP, AND BOAT BUILDER.

Fine FISHING SCHOONERS and YACHTS from Descriptive Design and Build

GASOLINE LAUNCHES A SPECIALTY.

MAHONE, - - - - NOVA SCOTIA.

OBED HAM SHIPYARD, 1920S

OBED HAM ADVERTISEMENT, 1907

Obed A. Ham was born in 1866 and lived the early part of his life in the United States, although his family was from Mahone Bay. After attending Acadia University, he returned to Mahone Bay and began his career in the shipbuilding business in 1896 by designing a schooner for the John H. Zwicker shipyard. By 1901 he had founded his own business and was both designing and building vessels. The Ham yard was located on the waterfront across the street from the Ham residence, which later became the Sou'Wester Bed and Breakfast. He specialized in yachts and cruisers, and became internationally famous for the quality of his work. Several of his boats became quite well known, such as four motor yachts in the "Cozy" series and *Gem*, which won the Coronation Cup at Baddeck in 1913. Clara Dennis claimed in 1925 that Obed Ham had designed and built 393 vessels. His yachts were so popular in the United States that Ham actually moved to St. Simon's Island, Georgia, for a while and built boats there, although he soon returned to Mahone Bay.

OBED HAM,
FIDDLER

Clara Dennis described Obed Ham as "the genius of Mahone" because, in addition to designing and building boats, he made violins and played them, was keenly interested in astronomy, wrote poetry, and even composed music. His best known composition was the song "Dear Old Mahone." Betty Berg, his granddaughter, remembers him as a very intelligent man but absent-minded and a dreamer—a "true artist" in her words. This photograph shows Obed Ham playing one of his handmade violins.

INDEPENDENCE, 1920s

South Shore schooners had always raced informally, but in the 1920s the sport became organized, with crews and vessels from Nova Scotia competing against their counterparts from New England. Captain Albert Himmelman was one of the most celebrated captains on the South Shore in the early 1920s, and was especially well known for his keen interest in schooner racing. After he lost the 1921 Nova Scotia championship, competing in *Independence* against Lunenburg's Angus Walters in *Bluenose*, he joined the *Bluenose* crew for the 1922 international race.

CAPTAIN ALBERT HIMMELMAN AND CREW ON *KENO*, 1923

After the 1922 international race, Himmelman had *Keno*, a 127-ton schooner, built by the McLean yard. It was designed not just to fish but to be the fastest schooner on the Atlantic seaboard. It was launched in the spring of 1923, but too late for that year's international race, so Himmelman again served on *Bluenose*. *Keno* disappeared in a storm in January 1924 after leaving Louisbourg en route from Newfoundland to Lunenburg, and it was speculated at the time that the ship's finely honed design had made it less dependable in stormy weather. Himmelman and seven crewmen went down with it. In this photograph Captain Albert Himmelman can be seen at the far right, and the mate, John Wilcox, in the front row, second from left.

OXEN HAULING ENGINE FOR *COTE NORD*, 1920

By the end of the First World War, it was apparent that the golden age of sailing ships was over and shipbuilders had to build motorized vessels in order to survive. Mahone Bay shipbuilders were slow to adapt, but the first vessel to be built with an auxiliary engine on the South Shore was the 147-ton schooner *Cote Nord*, built by the McLean yard in 1920. Mahone Bay's yards did well in the 1920s, partly because of the new rum-running business, which needed fast, motorized vessels. When Clara Dennis visited in 1925, the McLean yard had just completed *Silvia Mosher*, a forty-one-metre schooner, and *Marion & Emily*, a thirty-two-metre fishing vessel, and was working on another vessel for a Lunenburg firm.

The Burgoyne brothers merged their yards in 1924, and in May 1925 launched *Dominion Shipper*. Dennis reported that they had recently finished a 400-ton motor vessel, and two others were then under construction. This photograph shows six yoke of oxen pulling the engine down South Main Street to the McLean yard for installation in *Cote Nord* in 1920.

**ISLE MADAME,
1929**

The Ernst yard adapted as well. Willis Ernst told Clara Dennis in 1925 that his company was enjoying its best year since the war. That spring his yard had launched *Golden West II*, a 120-ton fishing schooner, and *Mark H. Gray*, a 165-ton schooner. Warren Eisenhauer, the yard foreman, declared that "the prospects are good for a big winter's work." In 1929 the company built the *Isle Madame*, a small ferry, for the provincial government.

***ESCADIL II*, 1920s**   Obed Ham's yacht-building business also thrived during the 1920s. Clara Dennis reported that "the sound of his hammer and saw still fill the air." Indeed, Ham built a new enclosed shed for his yacht-building business in 1924 or 1925, and his premises, it was reported, had "taken on a spic and span appearance since the painters have applied the brush with real artistic effect. All the buildings, including office, power house, workshop and drafting room and the covered building shed recently erected are resplendent in their dress of bright colour with large white lettering on both sides, visible to the passer by either by land or water, indicating the nature of the industry." Ham specialized in building luxury yachts for the American market. Dennis described "a luxurious boat" being built by Ham for a Florida client, twenty-one metres in length and costing $35,000, which was "the most elaborate yacht ever built in Nova Scotia." *Escadil II*, built in the 1920s, was typical of these vessels.

INDUSTRIAL SHIPPING COMPANY, 1942

The Great Depression of the 1930s, combined with the end of prohibition and the consequent decline of rum-running, had a brutal impact on the shipbuilding industry, and one is tempted to suggest that the death of Obed Ham in 1932 symbolically marked the end of an era. When the McLean and Ernst yards got contracts in 1933 that employed more than forty men, the *South Shore Record* proclaimed that they ended "a long period of idleness." But the Second World War brought a dramatic revival as wooden vessels—which could be built quickly and at relatively low cost—were needed to fill the gap left by the steamers conscripted into the navy or being sunk by German submarines.

There was also a need for specialized vessels, and in 1942 the Halifax-based Brookfield Construction Company acquired the Ernst yard to build freight barges and tugboats for the British Ministry of War Transport to accompany the troops in the planned invasion of Europe. Some five hundred men were employed, using assembly-line methods, and the Westhaver Oar Factory was contracted to produce forty-foot oars, or sweeps, for them as well This was not traditional shipbuilding, of course, and did not require the same skills. Even so, Mahone Bay could not supply that number of workers and some 250 men had to be brought in from Quebec and Newfoundland. They were housed in bunkhouses built behind the plant. The fact that so many of them were outsiders presented difficulties, however, as they apparently did not integrate very well into the community, and clashes between the workers and the locals were common.

Industrial Shipping also did some work on local contracts as well, building *J. F. Cowrie* in 1943. This was a significant event because *J. F. Cowrie*, which was built for the federal Department of Fisheries, was the first trawler to be built on the East Coast, although such vessels had been used for some years on the West Coast. The idea was to use it experimentally to determine if it was suitable for fishing on the East Coast. As one journalist explained, the great advantage of this new type of boat was that "it will tow thousands of yards of trawl and have the added advantage of speed in bringing in the catch." In the postwar years, of course, such trawlers became common and transformed the fishery.

DEMONSTRATION OF WARTIME BARGES, 1943

The barges built by Industrial Shipping were intended to accompany the troops when the invasion of Europe took place. They were built in six sections for ease in shipping. According to Ronald Crossland "back over the hill there was a mill that would produce all the lumber for these barges," and all the metalwork for assembly was done as well and shipped with the barges. These barges were the first sectional freight barges ever to be built anywhere, and W. F. Fletcher, the British Ministry of War Transport's technical director in Canada, chose the communities of Mahone Bay, New Glasgow, Parrsboro, Bouctouche, and Fredericton to do the work "because of their traditional skill in making wooden ships." They were designed by W. J. Roue, the Halifax marine architect best known for designing *Bluenose*. This rare photograph shows a demonstration of the barges for the British Ministry of War Transport and British, Canadian, and American army staff officers that took place at Mahone Bay in October 1943. As can be seen, the barge was powered by a large outboard engine, which was being tested for use, instead of having tugboats pull the barges.

MAHONE BAY SHIPBUILDING COMPANY, c.1944

Brookfield Construction also leased the McLean shipyard, which remained an autonomous operation under its new name, the Mahone Bay Shipbuilding Company, and produced Fairmile patrol boats and minesweepers for the Department of National Defence. In 1943 it erected a new building, which enabled it to carry out its construction in an enclosed environment; the first ship built in this building was *OK Service VIII*, a thirty-seven-metre freighter launched in May 1944. This photograph shows the Mahone Bay Shipbuilding Company's new sheds.

LAUNCHING *CT 61*, 1943

During the Second World War, ship launchings became common events once again. They had, the *Halifax Chronicle* reported on May 13, 1944, become "every day events of late" but were still "looked upon as something special by the town folks. They leave their daily tasks and young and old line the wharves for the show. Oldtimers can be found in groups reminiscing on the days when shipbuilding was Mahone Bay's chief industry." Here we see the town band, which led the parade to the wharf for the launching of *CT 61*.

LAUNCHING *TANAC V-254*, c.1944

This photograph shows the launching of *Tanac V-254* at Industrial Shipping sometime during the war.

MAHONE BAY PLYCRAFT FACTORY, 1949

After the war, Industrial Shipping became the Mahone Bay Plycraft Company, building pleasure craft with laminated plywood hulls. It was quite successful, producing as many as fifteen thousand shells a year, despite a fire in July 1956 that destroyed seven of the firm's eight buildings and two nearby homes, including that of its manager, Brigadier Arthur Roy. The company erected three new buildings along the Fauxbourg Road side of its Mahone Bay site to continue building shells, and three more buildings further down on the Main Street side of the property to finish them.

As the *Halifax Chronicle* noted, "a notable feature is that they are all consigned to the American market, which is in line with the government's policy of developing exports." Indeed, M. L. Robar, who was designer and superintendent in the 1950s, claimed in 1961 that during his years there the company built approximately 150,000 shells that were shipped to other companies to complete the boats, although the plant also produced about 1,200 completed boats annually as well. Increased competition in the American market, combined with a growing preference for fibreglass boats, soon made the plant unviable, and it ceased operations in 1962. This photograph shows men working on a number of partly completed boats in 1949.

ATLANTIC BRIDGE, 1960s

When Mahone Bay Plycraft closed in 1962, Industrial Estates, the provincial economic development agency, stepped in and arranged for the American Boat Building Company to take over the Fauxbourg site, which began producing "Paceship" fibreglass pleasure boats. In 1964 the company was acquired by Atlantic Bridge Company (ABCO), which built scallop draggers at the South Main Street site. It also took over the Paceship operation, but in 1975 it abandoned boatbuilding in order to focus on its industrial plastics operations. ABCO's decision to get out of boat production marked the end of commercial shipbuilding at Mahone Bay.

MCLEAN SHIPYARD FIRE, 1962

When Industrial Shipping's lease expired in 1950, the McLean yard reverted to its original name and continued to produce freighters and fishing vessels. Charles McLean died that year, and William carried on the business until he retired in 1961 and sold the business to Robert Zinck and Ray Leger. Supported by federal shipbuilding subsidies, they opened a subsidiary yard at Port Hawkesbury as well. Despite a major fire at the Mahone Bay site on May 19, 1962, they managed to build twenty-seven fishing vessels by 1967, when the subsidy program came to an end, putting 106 men out of work. The last vessel built by the McLean yard was *Liverpool Bay*, launched in 1967.

LAUNCHING A BOAT AT SMELTZER'S YARD, C.1950 Harris Smeltzer, who had taken over the Obed Ham Yacht Works, was joined in 1946 by his two sons, Philip and George, and continued to build cabin cruisers, yachts, and yawls. The shop had two levels. Smaller boats were built on the upper level and hauled out on trucks or on trailers pulled by tractors or horses. Larger boats were built on the lower level and were launched directly into the water. The company closed down in the 1950s, but its building survives; heading out of Mahone Bay towards Mader's Cove, it is the large red building on the waterfront before the Mader's Cove sign. This undated photograph shows Everett Ham with his horses helping to launch a boat for Harris Smeltzer.

**LEAMAN HIRTLE
AND WORKMEN
FINISHING A
YACHT, 1950S**

Born on July 29, 1910, at LaHave Islands, Leaman Harold Hirtle built his first boat, a dory, at the age of fourteen and went on to repair and build boats for local fishermen, first at LaHave and then at Halifax. In 1942 he decided to open his own shop, L. H. Hirtle Boatbuilder, in Mahone Bay, building lifeboats and repairing the rafts being built for war service. When the war ended and there was no further need for this type of work, he began building pleasure boats such as yachts and cruisers. At this point he renamed his company Nova Scotia Yacht and Boatbuilders Ltd., which was situated where the Save Easy grocery store is now. Most of the cruisers that he built were only partially constructed and then shipped by truck to Baltzer's Shipyard at Newburyport, Massachusetts, where they were completed. Hirtle employed as many as twenty-five men at peak times, but when he retired in 1959 the business closed. This photograph shows Leaman Hirtle and his workmen putting the finishing touches on one of his luxury yachts in the 1950s.

Chapter 3

Rum-Running Days

PATARA, C.1924

During the First World War, the temperance movement attained considerable public support, resulting in the passage of prohibition laws by Canadian and American governments between 1916 and 1920. Despite the fact that prohibition had strong public support in both countries, there was also widespread opposition, which led to a dramatic rise in bootlegging, especially along the Atlantic coast.

Initially, the vessels obtained their supplies directly from Europe and the Caribbean, but when a warehousing system was established on the French island of Saint-Pierre, just off the southern coast of Newfoundland, they began picking up their European supplies there. Nova Scotia's South Shore was obviously in an exceptionally convenient location owing to the proximity of Saint-Pierre, New England, and New York, as well the region's well-established tradition of hauling cargoes back and forth to the Caribbean islands.

Hauling cargoes of alcohol from the West Indies or Saint-Pierre was not an illegal activity as long as the vessels remained outside the twelve-mile limit on the government's offshore jurisdiction. What was illegal was the activity of those who ran fast motor vessels out to these so-called mother ships and brought the cargoes into shore, whether in Canada or the United States. But in the opinion of Hugh Corkum, who worked on rum-running vessels before becoming a police officer, "it is a misconception that there were many shady characters on the boats. All our crew were respectable family men of good character who had no feelings of guilt about what they were doing. They felt they were doing a job which gave them the opportunity to make a much better living than they could make fishing, freighting, or by their other previous occupation.... A great percentage of these men were highly respected in their communities, and all were on the boats because of their ability." Another veteran of the business later told folklorist Helen Creighton that "we were law-abiding, God-fearing Dutchmen and we weren't out to shoot or to steal a cent from anyone and if we came home on Sunday we'd all be at church."

In the beginning, rum-runners hired or purchased schooners that had been engaged in fishing or coastal freighting. Advertisements appeared in local papers offering cash for seaworthy vessels, and local entrepreneurs did not hesitate to enter this lucrative new business. According to Charlie Ernst, Willis and Selvyn Ernst, two of the three shipbuilding Ernst brothers, "decided to take the company's fishing fleet and head down to Turks Island and bring rum up and stay outside the twelve mile limit so that they were completely legal. Nothing illegal about it and then they had the fast boats come out and pick it up." Charlie's father, Arthur, who was a brother of Willis and Selvyn and had served as Mahone Bay's first mayor following incorporation in 1919, "wouldn't go along with that" and moved with his family to Pennsylvania in 1923, where he had attended college and married before returning to Mahone Bay. They returned to Mahone Bay in 1935 and that, according to Charlie, their youngest son, explains why "he was the poor member of the family and Willis and Selvyn had all the money." One schooner built by the Ernsts for rum-running was *Patara*, which was built in 1921. When it was sold in January 1924 to Halifax interests, the *Bridgewater Bulletin* claimed that it had been "one of the best sellers in the rum fleet, it being estimated that she sold during her career from 14,000 to 20,000 gallons of liquor."

While the impact of rum-running on the economy of South Shore communities like Mahone Bay is often exaggerated, there is no doubt that some men made a lot of money. Historian Ernest Forbes has pointed out that "at the primary level of distribution rum-running emerged less as a new industry than as a re-deployment of the resources of the fisheries." In other words, transporting liquor replaced fishing for many men and vessels. But the impact of this shift in activity was mixed. In May 1924 the *Lunenburg Progress-Enterprise* reported the closure of a fish plant because of the lack of fish, which it attributed to rum-running. At the same time, rum-running vessels employed smaller crews than fishing vessels, so while rum-running paid much better than fishing, the wealth was not as widely distributed. Writing as late as 1950, William Hirtle, a local educator, argued that the poor state of the local economy could be attributed at least partially to rum-running because "it drew attention away from the worth-while industries" during a difficult time when "it was necessary to devote all strength to the town industries if they were to survive."

As governments came to recognize the extent of public opposition to prohibition and the legal and social problems being generated by the illegal trade, they gradually modified their policies. During the 1920s all of the Canadian provinces except Prince Edward Island abandoned prohibition, replacing it with the government-controlled system that continues, albeit in a much more liberal form, to this day. The United States repealed prohibition in December 1933. Even so, rum-running continued for some years because the illegal product could be sold at a considerably more attractive price than what the government stores were charging for similar and sometimes diluted products. Still, the era of large-scale smuggling was over and with it ended a colourful period in the history of Mahone Bay and other South Shore communities.

COTE NORD, **1920s**   Enterprising Nova Scotians were not slow to seize the opportunity that prohibition so obviously presented, especially as economic conditions in both the fishing and shipbuilding industries were poor after the war, and significant profits could be made in the new business. Aubrey Backman later recalled that work on a rum-runner paid perhaps three times as much as fishing, plus bonuses. Hugh Corkum noted that not only were the men well paid, they "took pride in their ship and work." It was hardly surprising, therefore, when the US government calculated in 1924 that about one third of all the liquor being smuggled into that country came from the Atlantic coast, which became known as Rum Row, and that figure likely rose in subsequent years. No fewer than twenty-four fishing vessels were reported to have been sold to rum-runners. Indeed, the *Maritime Merchant* reported in 1925 that about half of the Lunenburg County fishing fleet was engaged in the rum trade, and Aubrey Backman believes that, considering the whole period of prohibition, the figure was closer to 75 per cent.

Two vessels built by the McLean yard that were used as rum-runners were *Norma P. Coolen*, a fishing schooner built in 1914, and *Cote Nord*, built in 1920. *Norma P. Coolen* was being used for coastal freighting when it was purchased at Halifax in 1924 by Captain Henri Ducos, who changed its name to *Cherie* and had it registered in France in the vain hope of making it exempt from Canadian and American regulations. It made several trips before it was captured off the coast of Maine in May 1925. *Cote Nord* was a 147-ton schooner with an auxiliary engine built in 1920 by the McLean shipyard for service on the St. Lawrence River and the gulf north shore. By 1927 it was rum-running under Captain John Randell, who working for the Makris syndicate, a family of Greek Americans in New York. In January 1928, while loading at Saint-Pierre, one of his crew, Nicolas Makris, got involved in a barroom brawl and shot and killed another sailor named Gustave Karlsen. Makris fled and escaped from Saint-Pierre on another vessel, and it was learned some years later that he had returned to Greece. Randell, incidentally, was later the captain of *I'm Alone*, whose sinking by a US Coast Guard cutter in the Gulf of Mexico provoked an international incident between Canada and the United States.

HARBOUR TRADER,
c.1928

Inevitably, given that rum-running generated large profits but also required capital and organization to succeed, especially as the Canadian and US governments strove to close it down, criminal organizations quickly got involved. Thus, while Nova Scotians fondly recall the excitement and adventures of these colourful seafarers of the 1920s and 1930s, we need to remember that they were for the most part employed by American criminal syndicates that were disreputable, to say the least. These syndicates could afford to buy or lease schooners and to organize the whole integrated operation from pick-up at Saint-Pierre to delivery at ports along the US east coast.

When the US Coast Guard acquired twenty-six surplus destroyers in 1924–26 to deploy against the rum-runners, the syndicates responded by ordering the construction of new and better vessels to replace the retrofitted schooners they had been using up till then. These vessels came to be known collectively as the banana fleet because they had a low profile resembling a submarine or floating banana. Construction of these vessels, which were very fast and sat low in the water, began in 1927 with *Harbour Trader* and *Standard Coaster*. More than one hundred rum-running vessels were built at various shipyards throughout Nova Scotia, at least five of them at Mahone Bay and six at Lunenburg. One old-timer claimed many years later that "in 1928 the main industry in Mahone Bay was building boats for rum running." As maritime historian D. A. Walker hastens to point out, "this was a legitimate, established and honest business which legally benefitted from prohibition, albeit perhaps with 'laundered' money." These vessels were not designed to carry cases of liquor. Rum came in small kegs but the other liquors were placed in six-bottle lots in canvas sacks and padded and jacketed with straw. These bags, which were known as "burlocks," were easily handled and stowed in the curve-sided holds, and the padding made for quiet transfers at sea with little breakage.

Standard Coaster was built at Liverpool, but *Harbour Trader* was built by the McLean shipyard in Mahone Bay. These vessels were designed to resemble ocean-going tugs with fenders all round and masts that could be lowered. Hugh Corkum, who served on *Harbour Trader* under his father, Captain George Corkum, later described it as "the pride of the fleet: majestic, streamlined, and one of the most notorious rum runners" on the South Shore. "The accommodations were exceptional for a ship of her period—two to a stateroom, all above decks—and she boasted a beautiful saloon directly below the pilot house. She had all the comforts of home." Not surprisingly, the ship's crew "were considered the cream of the crop." *Harbour Trader* made its first trip to Saint-Pierre in January 1928 under Captain Byron Ritcey, but Captain Corkum took command later that year. In all, it made about a dozen trips before it was captured near the entrance to New York harbour in December 1928. The ship was seized by the US government and the crew members were fined $500 each. The vessel was subsequently used by the US Coast Guard in New York harbour. This very rare photograph is the only known picture of *Harbour Trader*, other than one that appeared in a newspaper after its seizure.

SHULAMITE, 1931 *Shulamite* was built by the McLean yard in October 1930 and made only seven trips from Saint-Pierre to the American coast, carrying forty-five hundred cases on each trip, before its engines overheated and the vessel was laid up at Riverport through 1932 and 1933. Its sister ship was *Marvita*, which was built by the Ernst yard. Originally built as a regular cargo boat operating out of Liverpool, it was converted in November 1931 into a tanker. In the words of Geoff and Dorothy Robinson, historians of rum-running in the Atlantic provinces, "strangely enough there was no great local secrecy where the tanks were being built and installed." The tanks were taken from a Lunenburg-built vessel, *Winona R.*, because *Marvita* was 30 per cent larger.

When *Marvita* was ready to begin rum-running, Captain Arthur Himmelman, who had formerly commanded *Winona R.*, was made master. The Robinsons have documented twenty-one sailings from Saint-Pierre. As each load was approximately fifty thousand litres, this means that *Marvita* delivered more than a million litres of alcohol during its three-year career, making it one of the more successful rum-runners.

Ironically, *Marvita* was later purchased by the Newfoundland government, which used it as a revenue cutter patrolling against smugglers between Newfoundland and Saint-Pierre. *Shulamite* was also purchased by the Newfoundland government in April 1935 and used for customs work; it was subsequently taken over by the Canadian navy during the Second World War and used for a variety of coastal activities, until it was sold to two brothers in North Sydney who changed its name to *Norsya*. It was used for freighting but shortly afterward ripped a hole in its side on a submerged derelict and sank near Matane. Other prominent ships in the South Shore banana fleet included *Lomergain* and *Jacqueline M.*

CROSSLAND'S SERVICE STATION, c.1932

Rum-running insinuated itself into the culture and subsequent folklore of coastal communities like Mahone Bay. Many tales are told, mostly humorous, of rum-running exploits and the elaborate schemes devised for outwitting the police.

Ronald Crossland recalls one especially amusing story told to him by his father, who operated the Imperial service station that backed onto the inlet of the Anney River, near the war monument. The building sat on posts "and had a trap door that you could go in underneath the building. So Dad was down there doing the bookwork and he heard this commotion out to the side, and he went out of the room and looked out the window, and he saw these men carrying these kegs of rum out. He knew who they were, so he went out and he said, 'where are you getting that rum from? They said. 'under your building.' 'Under my building,' he said. 'Yes,' they said, 'we had hundreds of kegs stored under there over the time.' What they'd do when the mother ship came in, they'd always go out and meet the mother ship with small boats and bring it in, and it was where the river comes right up behind, and they'd come up there on high tides and then put it in there underneath the old service station to hide it until everything was clear and then the time came to deliver." This photograph, taken in the early 1930s, shows Crossland's service station, with Ronald Crossland's uncle Ellard on the right, behind his car.

DAVID ZINK WITH HEARSE, 1920S

Aside from hiding the liquor, of course, the rum-runners had to deliver it to their local customers. Bruce Joudrey recalls that "when they had anything worth transporting to one place or another, they resorted to all sorts of devices. Such as getting the use of a hearse and transporting it as a body, and of course they would have attire with tall high hats and nicely dressed up with bows, and they were lucky if on the way past the town police didn't salute. And I guess that was done more than once." Presumably they got the hearse from Zink's funeral home, which, according to Sally Thomas, writing in the *Bridgewater Bulletin* in May 2004, is the oldest surviving business in Mahone Bay. It was founded by David Zink in 1883 and remains in business today, still at its original site on Parish Street, although it is now called the Mahone Funeral Home. The hearse shown in this photograph may have been the one used in the above story.

SELVYN ERNST HOUSE, BUILT c.1900

Selvyn Ernst bought this fine home on the corner of Fairmont and Pleasant, just across the street from C. U. Mader's house, in the 1920s. Although Selvyn was a successful shipbuilder, he may have paid for this fine home, built around the turn of the century, at least partially with profits made in the rum-running business.

PICKELS HOUSE, BUILT c.1880

This magnificent house, called "Bayview," was situated on the present site of the Irving service station. It belonged to Dr. George A. Pickels and his wife Ann. Following her death in 1924, it was owned by Captain Maurice W. T. Wolfe, a sea captain who commanded *Shulamite* during its brief but highly profitable rum-running career. One wonders whether it was Wolfe's involvement in rum-running that made it possible for him to buy it. Following his death in 1951, his widow opened the house to tourists as the Edgewater Tourist Lodge. Until its demolition, this house was a visible reminder of the considerable prosperity that some Mahone Bay residents achieved from rum-running.

Chapter 4

Historic Homes

SECOND (NOW PLEASANT) STREET, 1912

Mahone Bay is one of the most picturesque and attractive towns in Nova Scotia. To a considerable degree this reflects its architectural heritage. Most of the buildings were constructed in the nineteenth century, although many survive from the eighteenth. In general they are in good condition, and many have been lovingly restored. With its combination of early New England influence and the popular architectural styles of the second half of the nineteenth century, Mahone Bay has become, in historian Ronald McDonald's words, "an aesthetically attractive and elegant community."

Few buildings from the early period have survived the ravages of time, although the sketches made by John Woolford and Henry Pooley when they visited Mahone Bay give us some sense of what the village looked like in 1818. And what is apparent is that it consisted of only a handful of residences scattered around the head of the bay, widely separated by fields and forest. Architectural historian Allan Gowans has described the dominant residential style in the early years as "brute functionalism." In other words, the settlers began by building small simple homes that could be erected quickly, using lumber planed at the local mills or brought in from New England.

It was not long, however, before the settlers replaced these early primitive dwellings with more solid structures. Because the South Shore of Nova Scotia was essentially a northern extension of New England, both economically and cultur-ally, it is not surprising that New England had a significant influence upon archi-tectural styles despite the fact that most of the original settlers were of German origin. Mahone Bay was not unique in this respect, of course, as the same is true of nearby Lunenburg.

Thus, many houses were built in the simple Cape Cod style, and, happily, sev-eral survive today. These houses, represented by the Christian Ernst and Valentin Wittman houses, were single-storey structures with a central hallway and fire-place. The Cape Cod style more generally familiar today—a two-storey building with two or more dormer windows—came later. Because there was virtually no Loyalist influence in Mahone Bay, the Georgian architectural style that flourished in other parts of the province is relatively rare, although one good example is the John William Kedy house, which was built in 1799. Kedy was not a Loyalist, but he was affluent and was no doubt influenced by the style then fashionable in other nearby communities and in England. This was an exception, however, and the simple Cape Cod style continued to predominate until about the 1860s, by which time the village had moved beyond producing agricultural products, lumber, and cordwood for Halifax to become a significant shipbuilding, fishing, and shipping centre. It is in the second half of the nineteenth century that we see the construction of larger and more ornate residences that were clearly influenced by popular architectural styles of the day—Italianate, Gothic Revival, Classical Revival, Picturesque, and Renaissance Revival. As well, Mahone Bay developed an ornate "gingerbread" style uncommon in the Maritime provinces, of which the Westhaver house is the best example.

CHRISTIAN ERNST HOUSE, BUILT c.1765

Possibly the oldest surviving house in the area is the Christian Ernst house, which sits high on the hill in Oakland with a magnificent view over the bay. Ernst (1724–98) was one of the first settlers at Oakland and built his first house near the water's edge. When he built this house a decade later, it seems likely that he dismantled his house in Lunenburg, brought the materials to Oakland, and reused them there. It is a classic early Cape with a simple wooden frame structure and a pitched roof, comprising one and a half storeys, with a centre door flanked by two windows on either side. The interior finishing in the parlour is exquisite with elegant moulding and a finely-detailed corner cupboard. The house remained in the Ernst family until 1939, the last owner being William G. Ernst.

WITTMAN HOUSE, BUILT C.1774

Valentin Wittman was one of the original settlers of Lunenburg in 1753. He was given land at Rose Bay, but resettled in Mahone Bay in 1754, where he received one of the original thirty-acre lots. In 1774 he acquired this lot and presumably built the house, which is an excellent example of the early Cape Cod style. It has been well preserved over the years and retains many original features, although two wings have been added in recent years. It is said to be haunted by the ghost of a small elderly woman who waits at the top of the stairs.

ZWICKER/MADER HOUSE, BUILT C.1775

Johan Georg "George" Zwicker (1742–1815) was a son of Johan Peter Zwicker Sr. (1710–89), who came from Zeiskam, Germany, on board *Gale*, and the brother of Johan Peter Zwicker Jr. ("Dr." Peter). When Mauger, Francklin, and Pernette began selling off their lands in 1774 (see Introduction), George Zwicker purchased the large block known as the Mauger's mill grant, and established himself as a miller. Although he subsequently sold a number of lots to regain part of his investment, he remained one of the largest landowners in the area. His home, a typical one-and-a-half-storey Cape, near the corner of West Main and Mader (now Orchard) Avenue, passed into the Mader family through marriage and was owned by John Mader from 1837 until his death in 1860. It remained in the Mader family for many years, but in recent years was known as the Old Settlers' Place Restaurant. Local tradition claims that there used to be a tavern in the cellar, and one can imagine men rowing up the nearby Anney River, tying up their boats, and strolling in for a mug of ale.

Later occupants have long claimed that the house was haunted by the ghost of Louisa, the daughter of John and Mary Mader, who lived there for many years until her death in 1929. One woman who lived in the house claimed that she once felt someone sit down on the bed beside her, and another time she felt as if someone was trying to choke her. At times a figure was seen in the hall, and one night the woman's children saw a woman standing at the foot of their beds. In 1978, when the house was being painted, an old key was found hidden in a tiny crevice under the hall stairs. Although it fit the entrance door, the owner left the key where he had found it. Shortly afterward a major fire all but destroyed the inside of the building and the owner found the key outside the front door! And Louisa's ghost has not been seen since.

The house appears to face Orchard Street, but that is actually the back of the building, which was, of course, built overlooking the bay. In later years the land between the house and the road was sold off and built upon, obscuring the view and requiring a back lane to be developed into Orchard Street. This photograph shows the Mader family posing before what was then the front of the house in the 1880s.

ALEXANDER KEDY JR. HOUSE, BUILT C.1777

Alexander Kedy Jr. (1746–1818) was one of two sons of Alexander and Ann Kedy. In 1777 he and his brother William (1744–1817) bought the Mushamush mill lands and the sawmill on the shore of the bay, as well as significant segments of the Clearland lots. According to Ned Harris, William "got out to Flake Island through drink and getting behind hand," and sold his interest in the lands to his brother in 1787 for £628, which made Alexander one of the largest landowners in the area. About 1777 he built this gambrel-roofed house, making it one of the oldest houses in Mahone Bay. Because of extensive renovations made to it over the years, it does not appear to be as old as it is, although inside it retains the original woodwork, brass hardware, and fireplaces. Harry Eisenhauer, who operated the Imperial service station and sold automobiles, bought the house in 1932 and added the verandah and full-length dormer.

JOHN WILLIAM KEDY HOUSE, BUILT IN 1799

Alexander Kedy Jr.'s son, John William Kedy, built this fine home next to his father's house in 1799. He carried on the family sawmilling business, and the family's growing prosperity is clearly reflected in this splendid Georgian structure, which can be seen in the sketches of Mahone Bay made in 1817 by the British artist John Woolford. Its appearance is deceptive; while it has a single central door, it is in fact a double house, a colonial duplex. Today, two side pavilions have replaced the six-foot square gabled porches which formerly gave an individual entrance to each side. Apart from that substitution, little change has been made since the house was built. There is a cooking fireplace on the ground floor of each side of the house, but the well in the cellar was shared, as was the curving stairway that leads to the parlours and bedrooms on the second and top floors.

When John William died, his will directed that his widow Catherine was "to enjoy the half of the house in which I now reside." His married son, also called John William, could continue to live in the other half, able to look out for his widowed mother and younger brother, Henry (b. 1819). John William Jr. later built a house on West Main Street and Henry continued to share this house with Catherine until her death in 1854. It remained in the Kedy family until 1945, then was empty until 1954, when Dana Sweeny restored it and established an antiques business there. Following the business's demise in the early 1980s, a restaurant and shops moved in. It has since been designated a provincial heritage property.

**KEZIA KEDY
SAMPLER, 1833**

People in Mahone Bay like to tell the romantic tale of John William Kedy, who died of a broken heart in 1850, a few months after the death of his favourite daughter, Kezia Catherine. The inscription on his tombstone reads, "As you are now I once have been/As I am now you soon will be/Prepare for death and follow me." Alas, John William was still very much alive and serving in the provincial legislature from 1847 to 1852 and did not die until 1874, possibly of a broken heart but more likely from old age. The confusion arises from the fact that there were many John Williams in the Kedy family, and one of them did die in 1850, but he was Kezia's uncle and he was seventy-five years of age. In any event, this charming sampler was done by Kezia when she was twelve years old. Kezia was only twenty-one when she died; as she had recently married Seth Millbury, she likely died in childbirth.

LONGACRES, BUILT C.1820

This simple but very attractive house is situated at the top of the hill on the Clearland Road, overlooking Mahone Bay. Its unusual front door, which features a reeded centre band, opens to show the narrow, enclosed quarter-turn staircase. The exterior of the house has a massive centre chimney with gabled roof design. The three large dormers, along with the new wing and porch, were added in 1931. In the parlour, outstanding for its fine woodwork with elaborate moulding between wall and ceiling, there is a delicately detailed corner cupboard with a keystone arch. Also in the parlour is a built-in wall cupboard with handsome reeded columns. In the old kitchen, now used as a dining room, there is a large fireplace and bake oven.

According to local legend, John William Kedy purchased the house from Jacob Burgoyne in 1831 as a wedding present for his son, John Henry. This seems improbable, as John Henry was only twelve years old in 1831 and did not marry until 1858. In fact, the house was purchased by George William Kedy, John William's brother, for his son, "Dandy" John Kedy, when the latter married Sarah Teal. Lillian Kedy (1879–1971), who lived there for many years, complicated its history further by claiming that it had been built in 1747. That too is highly improbable, as the area was not settled until 1754. It seems more likely that it was built in the 1820s. Lillian Kedy married John MacKenzie (1871–1968), and they eventually moved to Somerville, Massachusetts, but for many years they spent their summers at the old family home, which they operated as a bed and breakfast establishment until John died. In the 1950s it offered six bedrooms with three and a half baths, at three to four dollars per person per night. Despite the fact that she was married, Lillian was always known as "Miss Lillian Kedy." Following her death, the property was purchased by a local artist.

BLEYSTEINER/ MCLEAN HOUSE, BUILT IN 1848

John Bleysteiner, a sea captain, built this wonderful house on South Main Street in 1848, on a lot purchased from Benjamin Mader. The original house was built in the simple Cape Cod style with two-inch planks used horizontally and vertically for the frame, and one-inch solid stock sheathing inside and out. Sheets of birch bark were used for insulation.

John McLean, the shipbuilder, married John Bleysteiner's daughter Agnes in June 1861, three months after John Bleysteiner's death. He and Agnes lived in the house, along with Bleysteiner's widow, Ann, and raised their four children—Ella, Catherine, Charles and William—there. In later years McLean made substantial renovations to the house, reflecting his success as a shipbuilder. He raised the roof, added bay windows and a verandah, and installed a delightful triple-eyebrow arch over the front entrance. John McLean's son, William, who carried on the business until 1961, later lived here as well. This 1892 photograph shows John and Agnes McLean with some members of their family.

Left to right: Lenora Agnes Kaulbach (daughter of Ellen McLean, who had married John Creighton Kaulbach in 1880), Ann Bleysteiner, Charles, Catherine, Agnes, William, and John, in front of their renovated home.

**HILTON HALL,
BUILT C.1850**

Situated on South Main Street near the edge of town, this was originally the home of Benjamin Zwicker, who represented Lunenburg County in the provincial legislature from 1851 to 1855 before becoming collector of customs at Shelburne. One of his sons, Samuel, lived here in the second half of the nineteenth century. Another son, Alfred, also served as collector of customs at Shelburne, and was the father of Alfred Clairmonte Zwicker, a prominent local businessman and politician, and of Florence Zwicker, who married Ned Harris.

GREEN SHUTTERS, BUILT IN 1855

For many years Green Shutters was a well-known and much beloved tourism destination on the South Shore. Situated just outside of Mahone Bay at Mader's Cove, the house can be traced back to 1800 when Dr. Jacob Strum (1745–1840) and his family came to Mahone Bay and occupied a house on property belonging to Peter Zwicker Jr. ("Dr." Peter). A native of Germany, Strum had emigrated to South Carolina, but during the American Revolutionary War he sided with the British, serving as a colonel under General Cornwallis. In 1786 he settled at Shelburne as a Loyalist, and in 1800 he moved to Mader's Cove. His son John Peter (1788–1859) married Peter Zwicker's daughter, Ann Judith, in 1811, and a year later purchased the farm.

The original house was destroyed by fire in 1855 but was immediately rebuilt. It was substantially remodelled and modernized in 1932 by Laura Strum, Peter's granddaughter, who later opened it to the public as an inn. The old Dutch ovens, fireplaces, and wide plank floors were retained, however, and the house was furnished with antiques, including a handsome Sheraton grandfather's clock, which was one of the few items that survived the 1855 fire.

During the Second World War, Miss Strum was the Mahone Bay representative of the Ajax Club, a war charity founded by Nova Scotian women, that enabled many British sailors to enjoy a period of rest and rehabilitation at Green Shutters. From 1951 to 1963 Hilda Zinck carried on the business, which rightly claimed to have developed "a rather exclusive clientele, and has an enviable reputation for varied and delicious food, excellent services and every possible comfort." Indeed, the Green Shutters Cookbook, first published in 1959, remains a local favourite to this day. Zinck moved to Halifax in 1964, and the new owners, Mr. and Mrs. Eric Miller, eventually concluded that the building was structurally unsound for preservation. In 1972 it was torn down and replaced with a modern house, built in the traditional style, further up the hill from the water's edge.

BEGIN HOUSE, BUILT IN 1855

Benjamin Begin was a sailmaker who operated his business in the attic of his house on South Main Street and in the loft of C. U. Mader's warehouse across the street. He was succeeded in the business by his son Charles, who went into partnership with Obed Langille. Built in 1855 next to the lot on which Titus Langille later built his home, this house has a five-sided dormer, known as a Lunenburg bump, which descends into the front entry hall. The parlour ceiling was painted about 1895; it features a geometrically sectioned circle with dry brush scenes depicting the four seasons. There is also a marbelized parlour mantelpiece. The house is now home to the Mahone Bay Settlers Museum.

George Duncan House, built in 1861

George Duncan, a prominent merchant, built this house about 1861 on land that had belonged to John Mader. Across the road he had a wharf where he built several small schooners for his West India trade. The house remained in the Duncan family until 1960, when it was purchased by Eric and Vida Merchant, who operated what Will Bird described as "a unique shop that reflects the skill of Nova Scotian craftsmen with weaving and hooked rugs and pottery and wrought iron and carved wood." Known as The Teazer, it is, of course, named after *Young Teazer*, the legendary American privateer that exploded in the harbour during the War of 1812. The present structure is a reproduction of the original house, which was badly damaged by fire in 1971. It is a typical New England one-and-a-half-storey wooden structure with steeply pitched gables and pointed-arch windows in the Gothic Revival style.

J. H. ZWICKER HOUSE, BUILT c.1860

John Henry Zwicker, who became one of the largest shipbuilders in Mahone Bay, built this triple-gabled house in the 1860s on the corner of South Main and Fairmont Streets. Its steep three-gabled roof makes it one of the best examples of the Gothic Revival style in Mahone Bay. When Zwicker encountered financial difficulties in 1907, the house was sold to Edwin Kaulback.

WESTHAVER HOUSE, BUILT IN 1862

In 1860 a local carpenter, Benjamin Tanner, purchased two lots at the corner of Pleasant and South Main for £39. Clearly a shrewd businessman, he sold one of the lots to George Westhaver two years later for £150. Having bought the land, it seems likely that Westhaver hired Tanner to build the house as well. When George Westhaver died in 1925, his son Robert inherited the property and lived there until 1947. The original house was a much smaller structure, consisting of a storey and a half with a steep roof and a front door with sidelights and transom. Around 1900 George raised the roof, extended the back ell, and added dormers, windows, and the verandas. No doubt the fancy woodwork was done by the skilled workmen in his factory. Historian Ronald McDonald describes the house as "an extremely interesting example of Mahone Bay's unique gingerbread style."

TITUS LANGILLE HOUSE, BUILT c.1860

In 1856 Titus Langille, then a young shipwright, bought a lot on South Main Street from the Mader family. In the 1860s, after he had taken over Elkanah Zwicker's shipyard, which was directly across the road, he built this simple but impressive house. Titus and his brother Alfred married sisters, Caroline (1834–1884) and Mary Ann Berringer (1838–1865), at about the same time in 1861. Following Titus's death, his son, also called Titus (1862–1903), encountered financial difficulties in 1899 and could not pay his debts, so the house was sold at sheriff's auction for $235. Titus Jr.'s brother Obed (1868–1911), a sailmaker, bought it back two years later, although he had to pay $1,000 for it. It left the family again when Obed died, but Alexander Chisholm, the local merchant who bought it, immediately sold it back to Obed's widow, Nellie. She subsequently married Arthur MacKinnon, a sea captain, and continued to live there until 1955. For three years in the 1960s it was owned and occupied by George McVay, who operated the McVay fibreglass yacht-building company. It is now a private art gallery. This photograph shows Titus and Caroline posing in front of their home in the early 1880s. This house, with its simple clean lines, combines characteristics of both the Georgian and Regency styles.

SOUTH MAIN STREET, 1880s

This remarkable photograph shows Titus Langille's house at the far left. Next to it is George Westhaver's original house before the extensive renovations were undertaken. The building next to that is part of what became Bill's Store in the 1950s, now known as the Mahone Bay Trading Company.

SLAUGENWHITE HOUSE, BUILT c.1861

In 1861 Frederick Slaugenwhite, a carpenter, bought a lot on what later became known as Fairmont Street from Eleanor Mader, the widow of Benjamin Mader. He subsequently bought many of the surrounding lots as well, and controlled most of the land north of Fairmont, which was in fact known for a while as Slaugenwhite Street. Over the years he sold most of the lots, and at some point he built this fine house. Following Slaugenwhite's death the house was owned by George A. Mader, and then by his brother William M. Mader, who lived there until his mysterious death in 1933. His widow, Martha, remained in the house until 1954. It was then unoccupied for several years and deteriorated badly, but was renovated in the 1980s and returned to its rightful place as one of Mahone Bay's finer homes. An elegant structure, its most interesting and striking features include square projecting towers, decorative brackets, and Gothic transom windows around the front door.

**FAIRMONT STREET,
LATE 1880s**

This photograph of Fairmont Street, which was probably taken in the late 1880s, shows C. U. Mader's store and wharf at the end, backing onto the harbour. The white building at left centre, across the road from Mader's wharf, is Angeline Zwicker's Glasgow House hotel, on the present site of Abe Younis's furniture store. Next to it is Harriet Bruhm's house. The large dark house just up the road is the home of Frederick Slaugenwhite, the carpenter. The house at the end of the street, on the left-hand corner of Pleasant and Fairmont, was Mader's residence.

C. U. MADER HOUSE, BUILT c.1900

Mader later demolished his house and built a much larger one reflecting his business success on the same site.

OBED LANGILLE HOUSE, BUILT IN 1901

Titus Langille's son Obed built this fine double-eaved Gothic Revival house on Pleasant Street in 1901. It later became the Schnare home. This photograph shows Obed and his family posing for the camera.

GRAY HOUSE, BUILT IN 1879

Like C. U. Mader, Dr. Charles Gray decided to replace his house with a grander one, but unlike Mader he didn't inform his wife of the fact. As the story goes, following the death in 1872 of his first wife, Charlotte Snyder, who was the daughter of Rev. William Snyder, rector of St. James church, Charles Gray married Anna Louisa Rudolf, daughter of William and Matilda Rudolf of Lunenburg. When Anna returned to her family home in 1879 to wait out a difficult confinement, he decided to surprise her. He demolished their house and built a classic New England mansion complemented by an elegant Italianate triple-eyebrow transom over the front entrance. Thus, when Anna and their new daughter, Norah, were well enough to return to Mahone Bay, all that was needed were her finishing touches to the interior appointments. A second daughter, Annie, was born in 1886.

Dr. Gray had been practising medicine at Mahone Bay since 1858, and, according to the *Bridgewater Bulletin*, he was "a careful businessmen" who "had accumulated much wealth." Indeed, he held the mortgages on several properties in the town, and on at least one occasion he did not hesitate to foreclose on Captain James Henry Smeltzer when his ship was lost and the family fell on hard times. Nonetheless, he was regarded as "a good physician…and a friend to many a needy one." He was killed in 1897 when thrown from his carriage at Martin's River on his way to visit a patient. Anna died in 1925.

**MOVING A HOUSE,
c.1910**

It was not uncommon for houses to be moved in Mahone Bay. Even the Presbyterian church was moved from its original location on the hill down to Edgewater Road. Similarly, when the town hall moved to the Aberdeen Hotel, the old building was moved around the corner. And Charles Inglis chopped off half of his original building, which is now a separate structure on South Main, next to the former Zwicker's Inn. There are many other examples, as well, including the first train station and the original school. This photograph, taken by Fanny Ernst, shows four yoke of oxen moving a building in Blockhouse.

**E. A. ERNST
HOUSE, BUILT
C.1880S**

Not surprisingly, Edward A. Ernst, the "lumber king" of Mahone Bay, had a fine home built for his family, complete with exceptional detail-work, on West Main Street. Some claim that it was the first house in Mahone Bay with an indoor bathroom. Behind it there was a large barn and cooperage. Edward and Georgina Kedy Ernst had seven children, four of whom died young. The other three, all boys, achieved considerable success. Edward Alexander (1887–1967) carried on the family business and became Mahone Bay's first fire chief. William Gordon (1897–1939) was a Rhodes Scholar, served in the 85th Battalion during the First World War, and became a prominent lawyer in the town. He was elected to parliament in 1926, representing the Conservative Party, and was re-elected in 1930. He briefly served in R. B. Bennett's government as minister of fisheries in 1935, but was defeated in that year's election. According to Paul Ernst, he "was known to have had a problem with alcohol, and sadly took his own life in 1939." George (1905–65) became a clergyman, and after his retirement he and his wife purchased the Olive & Taylor Pharmacy on South Main Street, which they converted into an antiques shop. This photograph shows the Ernst home with Edward and Georgina in the cameo.

Chapter 5

Shops and Businesses

CONSTRUCTION ON SOUTH MAIN STREET

Because Mahone Bay's growth during the nineteenth century was driven increasingly by the shipbuilding and fishing industries, the town's commercial centre shifted gradually from what is now West Main Street, near the Kedy mill lands, to what is now South Main Street, fronting on the harbour. As well as shipbuilding, there were other industries, of course; most significantly, there were the Kedy and Ernst sawmills. There was also Westhaver's oar and block factory; an iron foundry; a planing mill; a box factory; a stove factory; shingle, tanning, and carding mills; and a smokehouse. In addition, there were two carriage shops, three hotels, three shoemakers, three builders, and five blacksmiths. Numerous other trades were also practised in Mahone Bay, such as sailmaking, masonry, caulking, pattern-making, net making, gunsmithing and tinsmithing, carpentry, ship carpentry, and construction. Along with these trades, by the 1860s about twenty-five retail outlets served the community: eleven dry goods shops, nine groceries, three hardware stores, two lumber supply dealers, and four general merchants. The town's prosperity was doubtless further stimulated when it was declared a port of entry in 1860. This meant that foreign vessels could now enter and leave Mahone Bay without first having to call at Halifax or Lunenburg.

DesBrisay, writing in the 1890s, described Mahone Bay as "busy," "rapidly growing," and "a rapidly improving village," and he predicted that "with a fine agricultural country in the rear, and excellent lumbering and shipping facilities, it must make still greater progress." Robert McLeod, author of *Markland* (1903), believed that Mahone Bay was "rapidly increasing in importance."

Commercial growth was not without its difficulties. An unsigned letter to the editor of *The Signal* in 1906 complained about the long hours that shop clerks were required to work. "We have to work in close confinement from 8 am to 9 pm, with slight intermission for meals." While a few stores had agreed to close three nights a week at 6 o'clock, most had not, and "a few busy body old women who sit all day thinking what to say during their nightly prowls, have been doing their utmost to destroy the chance of a further extension of the movement." Why could not every merchant, the writer asked plaintively, close his store "at sharp 6 o'clock three evenings a week, thus giving us clerks a chance for a breathing spell." It is not known if this appeal had any effect.

**ZWICKER'S INN,
1805**

Alexander Zwicker built his inn in 1805 on land granted to the Zwicker family, facing what later became South Main Street. The first house in what is now the heart of the town had been built nearby by Peter Zwicker Sr. in the 1760s. As we can see in this watercolour sketch by Henry Pooley—an officer in the Royal Engineers who went on to help build the Rideau Canal in the 1820s—the area was still quite undeveloped in the early nineteenth century.

Zwicker's Inn was a post house—a place where stage coaches could get fresh horses and their passengers could seek refreshments—on the road from Halifax along the South Shore, and was the first inn built between Chester and Lunenburg. The local militia allegedly stored their muskets in the attic for many years. Joseph Howe described it in 1830 as "a large comfortable Dutch house looking out upon a beautiful scene." And as Lord Dalhousie observed, the Zwickers were "most obliging & kind, anxious in the extreme to do anything in their power" to make his party comfortable.

When "Gentleman John" Zwicker got into financial difficulty in the 1850s, two of his sons, John Henry and Charles Augustus, acquired the property and subdivided it. John Henry, who was then beginning his career as a shipbuilder, subsequently built his triple-gabled house on the corner of South Main and Fairmont, and Charles took over the inn.

Beautiful Mahone Bay, N.S.

KEDY SAWMILL, c.1890

This photograph shows the Kedy sawmill at the mouth of the Mushamush River. It dated back to at least 1777, and its appearance probably did not change much over the next century. Alexander Kedy Jr.'s gambrel-roofed house can be seen in the centre of the picture, nestled against the hill.

ERNST LUMBER MILL, C.1890

By the early twentieth century "the chief man in the lumber business," according to Clara Dennis, was Edward A. Ernst. Indeed, he was known locally as the "lumber king of Mahone Bay." His company not only did the logging, but produced timber as well. Some of his timber was sold locally, but much of it was exported to the United States and the West Indies. Ernst later supplied the lumber for the barges built by the Ernst shipyard during the Second World War as well.

**VICTORIA HALL/
ROYAL HOTEL,
1855**

This building was erected in 1855 by Benjamin Mader, who soon sold it to Donald McDonald. The latter named it Victoria Hall. By 1857 it had become the Victoria Hotel, and when George Mader took it over some years later it became the Royal Hotel. When Sir Wilfrid Laurier stayed there, it had twenty-five rooms and charged $3 per day or $18 per week. When it was renovated in 1949, the *Bridgewater Bulletin* described it as "a hostelry that for years past still continues to maintain a service second to none." It closed in 1963 and subsequently became a senior citizens' nursing home.

G. A. WESTHAVER'S OAR AND BLOCK FACTORY, 1855

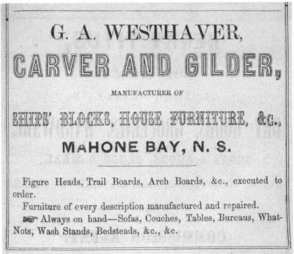

G. A. WESTHAVER,
CARVER AND GILDER,
MANUFACTURER OF
SHIPS' BLOCKS, HOUSE FURNITURE, &c.,
MAHONE BAY, N. S.

Figure Heads, Trail Boards, Arch Boards, &c., executed to order.
Furniture of every description manufactured and repaired.
☞ Always on hand—Sofas, Couches, Tables, Bureaus, What-Nots, Wash Stands, Bedsteads, &c., &c.

WESTHAVER ADVERTISEMENT, 1866

In 1855 George Alfred Westhaver founded an oar and block factory on South Main Street, where the Save Easy grocery store now stands. He is said to have been the pioneer in this business in the Maritime provinces. A remarkable man, Westhaver became well known locally for his beautiful wood carvings, gildings for vessels, house decorations, painting of banners and fine in-laid woodwork. He also invented and built machines with which to make oars. His son, Robert, who carried on the business, continued this tradition of innovation, inventing the "Perfect Spraying and Dusting Machine" that was widely used by fruit growers throughout the region. He also invented a portable elevator designed to lift the heavy barrels of apples out of the cellars of fruit warehouses. Clara Dennis claimed in 1925 that his machines had been exported to Australia, Florida, the West Indies, and even South Africa, "and it is surely a tribute to Nova Scotia that a little spot in a little province should produce things that are desired by other countries thousands and thousands of miles away."

BURGOYNE CARDING MILL, 1880s

At one time there were fourteen mills—saw, shingle, carding, and grist—on the Anney River, as well as a tannery. This photograph shows the Burgoyne carding mill in the 1880s with (left to right) Dawson Burgoyne, James Ernst, Lionel Zwicker, and Arthur Burgoyne.

JOSHUA ZWICKER SHOP, BUILT IN 1868

In 1868 Joshua Zwicker, a young merchant, built this combined home and shop across from his wharf, on a lot on South Main Street that had originally been granted to Nicolas Berghaus. The storefront is set in a conventional storey-and-a-half building with a pitched roof but, according to architectural historian Margaret Martin, "the shopfront is new for its time and place. For several decades trim had been vaguely Greek even in Lunenburg County.... The unknown carpenter used an attractive series of Italianate arches to link doorways and shop windows.... It was an idea admired enough to be repeated elsewhere in the village, but not with the delicacy exhibited here."

Zwicker was one of Mahone Bay's most dynamic young businessmen. In addition to selling dry goods, groceries, and hardware, he operated a lumber and shipping business. His promising career was cut short on March 19, 1871, when the schooner *Phoebe*, on which he was a passenger, capsized in a squall while entering Halifax and he was drowned. His widow, Mary, continued to operate the store for ten years, and Mariah Boehner later operated a china and glassware business there for more than fifty years. It now houses a real estate agency and law office. This branch of the Zwicker family seems to have had a tragic history. Joshua died at thirty-one years of age in 1871, Mary died at thirty-five years of age in 1883, and their daughter Cora died at nineteen years of age in 1888.

SLAUGENWHITE SHOP, BUILT IN 1875

The influence of Joshua Zwicker's building on Mahone Bay architecture can be seen in the house and shop built on West Main Street by Benjamin Slaugenwhite about 1875. It is a one-and-a-half-storey wooden frame building in the Greek Revival style, but the same Italianate influence can be seen in the graceful arched windows at the front of the shop. Slaugenwhite was a farmer and carpenter, and may have built the shop himself. This lot was originally part of one of the thirty-acre lots in the Clearland Division, but was purchased in 1787 by Henry Lantz. His descendants retained it until 1874, when Benjamin Slaugenwhite acquired it and built the shop. At some point in the twentieth century it became the property of John Lantz, who operated a grocery and furniture store. It is now the Amber Rose inn and antique shop.

C. J. INGLIS STORE, 1890s

In 1858 Charles J. Inglis and his wife Cassandra, who was a daughter of Elkanah and Catherine Zwicker, established a dry goods and grocery shop, with home attached, on West Main Street. This photograph shows the Inglis family outside the building in the 1890s. Cassandra is on the far left and Charles is on the far right. Next to Cassandra is their daughter Grace and her husband John Quinlan, and next to Charles is their son Percy. Grace Inglis attended private school in Halifax and became a teacher. She taught at the Mahone Bay Academy and married its principal, John Quinlan. They had a daughter, Clara, but when the marriage broke up as the result of a scandal, Grace and Clara returned home and John left town. Grace lived the rest of her life in the Inglis house with Percy, who became one of Mahone Bay's best-known characters. Clara lived in the family home until her death in 1988.

C. J. INGLIS STORE,
1912

As his business expanded, Charles decided to enlarge his premises. He removed the left-hand side of his shop, which was moved to South Main Street, then built a huge new structure over what remained of the original building. When completed it was the largest house in Mahone Bay. The interior is very elegant, with an imposing three-storey staircase, much elaborate wood trim, stained glass windows, and a wonderful fireplace lined with cast iron. After Percy took over the business, it specialized in fine china and attracted a wide clientele from all over Nova Scotia. He was skilled in lacework and rug design, and he was an avid gardener and flower arranger who supplied the flowers for many funerals. He was such an enthusiastic antiques collector that the shop overflowed with treasures that were on display but not necessarily for sale. Old-timers recall that Percy liked to give tours to visitors but seldom invited local people in because his collection had primarily been acquired from them. Percy and Grace liked to entertain, hosting card games in the parlour and even offering dance lessons in the third-floor ballroom.

After Clara died the house and shop were sold to Suttles and Seawinds, a company founded by Vicki Lynn Bardon that handsews unique clothing that is sold internationally. A 1993 profile of Rudolf Nureyev in *Elle* magazine showed the famous dancer wearing a Suttles and Seawinds jacket that he had purchased in New York in 1985. This photograph shows the enlarged building as it appeared in 1912.

C. U. Mader store, c.1900

Charles Uniacke Mader was one of Mahone Bay's most successful businessmen. Born in Mader's Cove, he was the great-grandson of Bernard Meder, one of the original German settlers in the area and the man for whom the cove is named. At the age of fourteen Charles went to work as a clerk in a Mahone Bay general store, and ten years later he opened his own establishment. By the end of the century he owned eight vessels, which fished and engaged in coastal freighting. In the autumn, for example, they would take apples and cabbages up and down the coast to various villages and to Prince Edward Island, bringing back potatoes, turnips, pigs, and geese. Mader's store outfitted his ships but served the general public as well.

Mader was very active in the community, serving on the school board, on the management board of the poorhouse, and as secretary of the agricultural society. He was the most prominent Liberal in Mahone Bay for many years, serving as president of the Lunenburg County Liberal Association and representing the area in the provincial legislature from 1904 to 1911. When he retired, his son, Frederick Uniacke Mader, carried on the business. This fine photograph shows Mader's store about 1900 with him posing proudly in front (in suit). To the left can be seen part of his wharf and storehouse. The old gentleman to his right with the cane is his father, John Francis Mader, who was about ninety years of age at the time.

Dominion of Canada.

Agreement with Fishermen.

NAME OF SHIP.	OFFICIAL NUMBER.	PORT OF REGISTRY.	Port No. & date of Register.	Registered Tonnage.
Schr Maimie Dell	112712	Lunenburg	No 9 April 14 1903	97 67/100

REGISTERED (MANAGING) OWNER.		MASTER OR SKIPPER.	
NAME.	ADDRESS, State Number of House, Street & Town.	NAME.	ADDRESS, State Number of House, Street & Town.
C. W. Mader	Mahone Bay N.S.	John W. Westhaver	Mahone Bay

It is Agreed between _C. W. Mader_ agent or owner of the Schooner _Maimie Dell_ now ready for carrying on the BANK and other FISHERIES of the Dominion of Canada or Newfoundland, and _J. W. Westhaver_ Master or Skipper of the said Schooner, and the Fishermen whose names are to this agreement subscribed, that the said _C. W. Mader and Owners_ will, at their own expenses, equip the said Schooner _Maimie Dell_ with all the necessary tackle and apparel for a fishing voyage or voyages ; the provisions, salt and craft shall be provided and paid for by _C. W. Mader and Owners_ and that the said _John W. Westhaver_ Master or Skipper, with the said Fishermen will pursue the Cod and other Fisheries, in the Schooner _Maimie Dell_ during the present fishing season, and will use their

MADER CONTRACT, 1903

Mader's business records are preserved in the Settlers Museum and show that much of his business was conducted through bartering and lines of credit to his employees. Little cash was ever paid out. Mader contracted with sea captains, in this case John W. Westhaver, to sail his vessels in exchange for a share of the profits. *Maimie Dell* was a ninety-seven-ton fishing schooner built for Mader in 1903 by the Burgoyne yard.

A. C. ZWICKER'S BUSINESS, 1890S

Although Monte Zwicker's business, which was on the corner of West Main and Mader (now Orchard) Avenue, looks like a shop, in fact, as his obituary said, his business interests were "many and varied." Among other things, he rented horses and carriages, and handled deliveries to and from the nearby railway station. By the turn of the century this building had become the American House, a boarding establishment operated by C. W. Joudrey. W. H. Longley, who was principal of the high school in 1904–06, stayed there, as did Captain Ben Westhaver. Longley enjoyed his walks and talks with the old sea captain, but was less amused when his umbrella and gloves were stolen from the front hall.

Dail Millett's mother later had an ice cream parlour there, and for some years it was the Blue Boy Restaurant. The building is still blue today, but unfortunately is in a state of serious disrepair. The Aberdeen Hotel is behind the house on the left. As can be seen in this photograph, the building was originally a storey higher with a peak, but the upper level was removed following a fire.

AD FOR AMERICAN HOUSE, 1907

CHISHOLM SHOP, 1890s

Not much is known about Alexander Chisholm, although he obviously was a friend of the Langille family. Born in 1848, it seems likely that he was not a native of the Mahone Bay area, as he seems to have been the only Chisholm there in the late nineteenth century. As well, he was Catholic, so he may have moved to Mahone Bay from eastern Nova Scotia. He was a dry goods merchant with an impressive store on West Main Street that had elegant rounded glass windows. Because he never married, he boarded for many years with Caroline Kedy.

Warren H. G. Hirtle began working for Chisholm in 1901 for $15 a week, and when Chisholm died in 1916, Hirtle bought the business and operated it as Hirtle's Dry Goods until 1960. At some point in the early 1920s he moved the business to the corner of South Main and Clairmont. Years later he recalled Chisholm as being a very public-spirited citizen who took a keen interest in the town band. Indeed, he supplied the entire group with new instruments on one occasion, and over a period of time bought uniforms for every member. Chisholm's shop, which no longer has the rounded windows, later was a doctor's office.

PICKELS'S DRUG STORE, 1891

In 1891 George A. Pickels bought a lot beside the Anney River that had originally been part of the Mauger's mill land grant. He moved a building across the road from what is now the site of Dr. Robert Ernst's dental office, and this building, which had been erected sometime between 1850 and 1865, became his pharmacy. Following his death it passed through a number of owners but continued to be a pharmacy, and was known for many years as the Olive & Taylor Pharmacy as it was owned by Drs. Allan Olive and Catherine Taylor. The first office and terminal of the local telephone company, which had been founded in 1886 by F. E. Wade, was in the back of the store. Orren Joudrey, who worked in the pharmacy, was also responsible for operating the switchboard and collecting the quarterly telephone bills.

In 1964 Rev. George Ernst and his wife Ann acquired the building and converted it into an antiques shop. This building, which has changed very little over the years, although Gregory Grammer restored it to its present elegant state when he operated it as a bookstore, is a very good example of Classical Revival architecture with its front gable plan. Other interesting features include returned eaves, classical moldings, heavy entablature, and flat attached pilasters. This 1891 photograph of the shop also shows people standing above the nearby falls on the Anney River.

AMBROSE EISENHAUR'S CARRIAGE FACTORY, c.1910

Ambrose Eisenhaur's carriage factory was situated on the inlet of the Anney River, facing the Main Street intersection across from George Duncan's house, which is now the Teazer gift shop. Magnificent carriages and sleighs were built here and shipped all over Canada. They were painted, stencilled, and wood-grained by Nathaniel Langille, who lived across the street from the factory. In the early years of the twentieth century, despite the invention of the automobile, Eisenhaur reported "having lots of work on hand." At the end of June 1909, for example, he delivered a three-seated light buck to George Mitchell in Chester and a top buggy to Joseph Wyman in Bridgewater. The *Progress-Enterprise* reported they had a "natural wood finish and certainly looked nice." In 1915, adjusting to the times, Eisenhaur fitted Lunenburg County's first passenger bus for the Lunenburg-Riverport Busline. This photograph shows Eisenhaur's carriage factory with (left to right) Harry Eisenhaur, Ambrose, Guy, and Philip Mader Eisenhau[e]r.

EISENHAUR'S SERVICE STATION, 1940s

In the 1920s Ambrose Eisenhaur opened a garage that serviced automobiles. He also sold Imperial gasoline. When Ambrose died the business was carried on by his two sons, Harry and Guy. Harry bought Guy out in 1927, and began selling cars, acquiring the Nash dealership. About 1929 he sold the service station business to Freeman Crossland, who built a station next door. Harry's son Philip carried on the car dealership, becoming the dealer successively for Hudson, Studebaker, and finally Hillman cars. At some point following his retirement in 1952 the old building was demolished. This photograph shows Philip Eisenhaur standing in front of his business in the 1940s.

**GLASGOW HOUSE,
c.1910**

After Charles Augustus Zwicker died in 1904, his widow Angeline opened a hotel that she called the Glasgow House, assisted by her daughter Millie. It has been claimed that the Glasgow House illegally served liquor and was charged several times with bootlegging, although the 1907 town directory indicates that it was licensed to sell alcohol, and it has even been claimed that the Glasgow House may have been a brothel at one time. Whether or not any of these charges is valid, Angeline Zwicker did maintain a showroom at the side of her hotel where travelling salesmen displayed their goods for local merchants.

ANGELINE ZWICKER, 1910

In addition to running a hotel, Angeline Zwicker was a keen gardener, who, as an old lady, often offered flowers to passing children to take home. In this photograph she is proudly showing off her garden to the photographer. Note the many conch shells brought home by sailors from the West Indies.

**LAURIE HOUSE,
c.1905**

This building, erected in 1848, was Ebenezer Frail's hotel from 1874 to 1882, then James B. Millett's hotel from 1884 to 1900. James and Rosena Langille operated it as the Laurie House from 1904 to 1910. This photograph was probably taken in the winter of 1904–05 as the livery stable next door still bears the name of J. B. Millett's hotel. From 1910 to 1924 the Penney family operated it as the Aberdeen Hotel.

MILLETT'S STORE, C.1900

MILLETT AD,
*SOUTH SHORE
RECORD,* MARCH
29, 1934

Freeman Millett's popular millinery store was next to J. B. Millett's hotel and livery stable until it burned down.

Main St. and Bank of Montreal, Mahone Bay, N. S.

BANK OF MONTREAL, c.1912

The Bank of Montreal opened a branch in Mahone Bay around the turn of the century, in a new building that now forms part of the Mahone Bay Trading Company. In 1911 it moved down the street to its own building, erected on land purchased from Freeman Veinot. Titus Langille had owned the land for a while, but in 1868 he sold it to his brother Alfred, the tinsmith, who built a house there, across from his factory. Freeman Veinot bought it in 1892, but sold it to the bank in 1910 when he decided to move to Massachusetts. The bank quickly became the centre of financial activity in Mahone Bay and continues to be a well-known landmark on the local scene. As historian Ronald McDonald rightly observes, "its pleasing appearance and neo-classical features make it one of the most attractive buildings in Mahone Bay."

**HYSON'S SHOP,
1920S**

Hyson's "Fancy Groceries" store was one of the town's best loved businesses for many years. It was operated by Reginald Edward Hyson (1874–1949) and his wife Helena (1887–1964). Reg also represented the Sun Life Assurance Company in Mahone Bay, was manager of the General Finance Corporation, and headed the group that established the *South Shore Record* in 1932. Many older residents will especially remember how beautifully the shop windows were decorated at Christmas, a memory that Alice Hagen, the artist and potter, captured in a wonderful picture. Reg and Helena had a son, Herbert (1919–2002), who lived most of his life above the store, and in his later years became the town's unofficial historian. This photograph shows Reg showing off his new car in front of the store. The window display is featuring "red wine grape juice."

SOUTH MAIN STREET, 1912

This photograph of South Main Street in 1912 shows C. F. Zwicker's meat market on the right.

SOUTH MAIN STREET, C.1936

This fine photograph, taken in the middle 1930s, shows Reg Hyson's shop on the left, and on the right Hirtle's dry goods shop, Schnare's, W. H. S. Zwicker's dry goods shop, and E. A. Wile's jewellery store. The Zwicker and Wile shops were sold in the 1950s to Bill Webber, who joined them to create Bill's Store. The post office, which was built in 1935, cannot be seen, but is between the Hirtle and Schnare shops.

Chapter 6

The Churches

MAHONE BAY'S FAMOUS THREE CHURCHES, C.1907

When Lunenburg was first settled, there were three main religious denominations. In order of popularity, they were Lutheran, Presbyterian, and Anglican. Although Lutherans were the largest group, the Anglicans had the advantage of being members of the established church that received state support. It was hardly surprising, therefore, that the first church built in the area was an Anglican church, St. John's, which was built in 1753 when Lunenburg was first settled. Lutheran and Presbyterian churches soon followed, in 1769 and 1770 respectively.

The people of Mahone Bay were served for many years by the Lunenburg clergy, who visited from time to time, holding services first in houses and then in the school, as well as by lay preachers like "Dr." Peter Zwicker of Oakland. They also sometimes attended services at the churches in Lunenburg. While some could no doubt travel by boat, most had to walk the twelve kilometres each way over rough roads. According to local tradition, people walked barefoot, carrying their shoes until they reached the outskirts of town, in order not to wear them out. Clearly this was unsatisfactory, and it was inevitable that as the population grew, churches would be built at Mahone Bay as well.

ST. JAMES ANGLICAN CHURCH, BUILT IN 1833

There is considerable confusion over which was the first church in Mahone Bay. It is usually claimed that the Union and Harmony House was the first because it held its first service in September 1834, whereas John Inglis, the Anglican bishop, did not consecrate St. James until July 1835. However, Inglis had visited Mahone Bay on June 7, 1826, to approve the proposed site of the church at the Mushamush burial ground on Clearland Road, overlooking the head of the bay. He arrived on the brig *Chebucto*, which had been lent to him by the Admiralty to enable him to tour outlying coastal settlements. Accompanied by a large delegation from the village, he was impressed by both the location and the enthusiasm of the people. The church was built on land that was originally part of the Mauger-Zouberbuhler grant, which was acquired by George Zwicker in 1777, and later by John William Kedy. Kedy donated it to the church on June 3, 1833, apparently some time after construction had actually begun, as the building was completed only a month later. Rev. James C. Cochran of Lunenburg held the first service there on July 14, 1833, preaching on the theme, "This is none other but the House of God, and this is the gate of Heaven."

The church may have been completed but it was pretty basic. A galleried Georgian-style building, its original pews were boards placed on heavy blocks of wood, and the walls were only single-boarded for a long time, making the building drafty. Indeed, it was reported that at the funeral of Anna Zwicker on December 3, 1833, snow drifted through the walls onto the congregation. A few months later, on May 25, 1834, the congregation decided to finish the chapel, and agreed that any person who contributed £2 to the finishing of the pews was entitled to possess and enjoy one pew forever, to be passed on to their descendants if they continued to reside in the township. The two double pews were readily purchased for £4 and it was unanimously agreed that at funerals the block of pews immediately in front of the pulpit was to be occupied by the mourners. At the same meeting Ezra Ernst was re-engaged as sexton at a salary of £2 a year, with instructions to sweep the floor once a month. The chapel was consecrated on July 7, 1835, by Bishop Inglis, who was joined at the service by Rev. T. T. Moody, the missionary at Liverpool; Rev. Joshua Weeks, the missionary at New Dublin; and Rev. James Shreve, the missionary at Chester.

It is, therefore, difficult to determine if St. James was "completed" before or after the Union and Harmony House. A bell weighing 170 kilograms was purchased in Boston for £34; the *Colonial Churchman* declared on June 1, 1837, that "the tone is good, and it was first used Sunday last." By 1858 the chapel had become too small for the growing congregation and it was cut apart and greatly enlarged. Some years later a square tower was added.

UNION AND HARMONY HOUSE, BUILT IN 1835

The second church built at Mahone Bay was the Union and Harmony House, which served the Baptist, Lutheran, Methodist, and Presbyterian congregations. It was located on a small lot purchased from Henry Zwicker, who had inherited land from the original Mauger-Zouberbuhler grant. The church building still stands near Bayview Cemetery, next to the George Kedy house. Construction began in 1833, and the first service took place in September 1834. The original trustees were John Andrews (Baptist), Peter Strum (Lutheran), Frederick Mader (Methodist), and Valentine Zwicker (Presbyterian). As their congregations grew, the various denominations built their own churches, and the building was sold in February 1874 to Gabriel Slauenwhite and James Hyson, who converted it into a duplex home. It was later owned by Snyder Slauenwhite, who used part of it as a harness workshop, and in recent years it has been occupied by Dr. Ken Gregoire. Despite extensive renovations over the years, one can still see the original floors in one of the bedrooms, with markings still showing the place of the original pews.

PRESBYTERIAN CHURCH, BUILT IN 1863

By 1860 the Presbyterians felt that they needed their own church and therefore built one from 1861 to 1863 at the top of the hill on the Clearland Road, next to St. James. As Ned Harris described the situation in 1884, the Anglican and Presbyterian churches were "back to back" on the hill. "There is no fence between, a burial ground all around. We go past the Presbyterian into ours. They have a hill all to themselves." The Presbyterian church—which seems never to have been given a name—was built in the Gothic Revival style with a steeply pitched roof.

It remained a Lunenburg charge until 1869, when it became autonomous. The first minister was Rev. Ebenezer McNab, who was paid $300 per year plus a supplement of $120. The call to McNab was signed by all forty-three members and adherents of the church. The first elders were George Eisenhaur, Alexander Kedy, Jacob Kedy, John William Kedy, John McKinnon and George Zwicker. Alexander Kedy was treasurer and Katie Kedy did the bookkeeping, later succeeding her husband as treasurer. This rare photograph shows the Anglican and Presbyterian churches at the top of the hill, as they appeared in the early 1880s. The Presbyterian church is on the right.

PRESBYTERIAN CHURCH, 1894

McNab seems to have been a hard worker; it was reported in 1870 that he preached faithfully, had five bible classes with an average total attendance of about a hundred, visited the flock, attended church courts, administered the sacraments regularly, and supervised the youth and Sunday school work. By 1877 the congregation had grown to a hundred families with sixty pupils in the Sunday School. The congregation was lax about paying his salary, however, and he seldom if ever received the full amount promised in any year. This was one of the reasons why he left in 1877. But when his replacement, Rev. D. Stiles Fraser, arrived, he discovered to his horror that McNab had never kept any records of births, marriages, or deaths!

In 1878 a church bell was purchased for $60. Meanwhile, land at the bottom of the hill had been purchased in 1871 from Louisa Mader, John Mader's daughter, for $360, and the manse was built at a cost of $1,551. Jacob Kedy supplied the pine boards for the interior work. It was completed in 1872 and painted a dark buff colour with darker trim. George Eisenhaur (1811–92), who, according to one account ran the church "almost single-handed, except, of course, for the assistance of the Almighty," was the chief purchasing agent for materials and also held the mortgage for the amount owing on the manse, $781.05, when it was completed. This mortgage was never paid off, and in the spring of 1889 he forgave the debt.

An amusing story is told about George Eisenhaur. One year, when the church needed some means of lighting for evensong, a meeting of the elders was called. Eisenhaur, of course, presided. When one timid soul suggested that they might purchase a chandelier, he allegedly jumped to his feet and shouted, "The hell ve vill, ve haven't anyvon who can play vun." This anecdote highlights the fact that for several years there was no organ, and the singing was led by Henry Eisenhaur of Mader's Cove. He was succeeded in the 1880s by George and Augustus Kedy, who served until 1885, when an organ was purchased. Lavinia Kedy was the first organist.

In 1885 the Presbyterians decided to move their church down the hill, next to the manse. Needless to say, this was an enormous task, and it took ten days to complete. The operation was carried out by J. B. Chute & Son of Bear River, and the church made the four-hundred-metre journey down the hill without sustaining any damage, despite a severe storm during which Fraser reportedly stayed up all night praying for its safety. The cost of the move was $465 for the new foundation and $140 for Chute's services and other expenses. The old church site was sold for grave lots at $1.50 each, however, and the $449 raised almost paid for the move. Some believe that this undated photograph shows the church raised on cribwork in preparation for its move down the hill in 1885, but it more likely shows the church when it was raised in 1894 to enable the construction of a basement, which included a church hall.

ST. JOHN'S LUTHERAN CHURCH, C.1870

As Anglican Bishop Inglis noted in his diary in July 1835, "most of the inhabitants of this thickly populated area are Germans and their descendants. Many of them are pious Lutherans, who delight in the service of our church," and he was, of course, hopeful that they would attend St. James. It was not to be. When the Union and Harmony House no longer met the needs of the growing congregation in the 1860s, a new church was built in 1869, on a piece of land purchased from John Mader for $64. St. John's was the first church to be built on the road at the bottom of the hill, facing the scenic waterfront. This photograph shows the original church as it appeared in the 1870s.

LUTHERAN CHURCH, c.1905

The Lutheran church underwent extensive renovations in 1903, which included adding the side wings, placing amber stained glass windows in the chancel, and adapting the tower to accommodate a bell. At the same time, the Sunday school room and church hall were added. The 1903 building is beautifully proportioned, and the sanctuary is serene and conducive to worship. At the back of the church is a large regulator clock facing the pulpit, intended perhaps to be a gentle reminder that brevity is the soul's delight. The first visiting pastors were Rev. C. E. Cossman, who served in German, and Rev. W. W. Bowers, who served in English. Rev. J. A. Scheffer, who came in 1876, was the first pastor to minister in both languages. The parsonage on South Main Street was built in 1890. This photograph shows the church as it appeared after the renovations in 1903.

METHODIST CHURCH, BUILT IN 1874

The first Methodist church in Lunenburg was built in 1816, and by 1818 it had a membership of eighty-six persons. In 1821 Rev. William Black, minister of the Brunswick Street church in Halifax and the father of Methodism in Nova Scotia, spent several weeks at Lunenburg, preaching twice each Sunday, with George Orth translating his message into German. One Sunday, Black reported, he administered communion to about one hundred people, all but ten of them from the rural areas, including Mahone Bay. Methodist services were held there as early as 1822, probably in people's homes, outdoors, or in barns. From 1833 the Methodist congregation met at the Union and Harmony House, but land was eventually purchased from Joseph and Leonard Young for $200, and in 1872 construction began on a church at the corner of Maple and Fairmont Streets. The cost of construction, $2,700, was defrayed by selling pews.

The first service took place in 1874, conducted by Rev. Thomas Rogers. The first visiting minister was Rev. C. Lockhart. Mahone Bay remained part of the Lunenburg Circuit until 1884, when it became autonomous. The first resident minister was Rev. Alban Daniel, who was a probationer, and he was succeeded by other probationers until Rev. J. L. Batty arrived in 1887 as the first ordained minister. Extensive alterations were made in 1904–05 when electric lighting was installed, the chancel was built, and the stoves were replaced by a furnace.

BAPTIST CHURCH, BUILT IN 1875

Mahone Bay's Baptist congregation began in 1809, when a committee from the Baptist churches of Newport (Windsor) and Chester met at Lunenburg at the request of a number of Baptists in Northwest Range to assist in organizing a church. A congregation was founded that met in members' homes until 1819, when they agreed to erect a building and subscriptions were solicited. Rev. Joseph Dimock of Chester served as visiting minister. The Baptists began holding regular services at Mahone Bay in the Union and Harmony House, then in a hall owned by Joseph Hamm on South Main Street, until they built a church on Maple Avenue in 1874–75. The first service took place on March 14, 1875, with Rev. Dr. E. M. Saunders, the eminent Maritime Baptist historian, preaching the first sermon. The first visiting pastor was Rev. R. S. Morton, and the first resident pastor was Rev. A. E. Ingram. The Baptist congregation became autonomous in 1907. In 1911 the church hall was added to serve the recreational needs of the congregation and to house the Sunday school, which had been active since 1860. Nathaniel Langille painted scenery for the stage.

REV. WILLIAM HENRY SNYDER, c.1880

Although they had a church, Mahone Bay's Anglicans did not have a priest in the early years. As Bishop John Inglis noted in his diary in July 1835, "the people here, altho they are receiving much attention from the Missionary at Lunenburg, are desirous of having a clergyman of their own and as the congregation is very large it is desirable that their wishes be gratified."

It was another decade, however, before Rev. J. Philip Filleul was appointed the first resident missionary at Mahone Bay. He was succeeded in 1852 by Rev. William Henry Snyder, who served until his death in October 1889, except for a brief absence in 1874–75. A native of Shelburne of Loyalist descent, he was of mixed English-German ancestry: one of his ancestors came from Heidelberg and was governor of Pennsylvania, while his great-grandfather on his mother's side had been a British admiral. He was ordained in 1836 and served as curate in Lunenburg and as resident missionary at Weymouth prior to going to Mahone Bay. He was popularly known as "Parson Snyder" and Ned Harris described him in 1884 as "a jolly old fellow" who "is never tired of talking, spinning yarns all the time." He married twice and produced twelve children, seven of whom pre-deceased him.

Snyder had a sometimes turbulent relationship with his congregation. It was the custom for the congregation to supply free firewood to the rectory, and it is recorded that on January 6, 1860, 115 yoke of oxen were required to haul the firewood for Snyder's use. When this proved to be more than he needed, he shipped six cords to his son-in-law in Saint John, much to the displeasure of many of his parishioners who thereafter refused to supply him with any more. On another occasion when he was delivering a fiery sermon on "hell and demons" a hard-of-hearing parishioner in the back pew jumped up and declared fervently, "Parson Snyder, Parson Snyder, there are just as many Snyders in hell as there are Demones!"

**NED HARRIS,
C.1900**

Ned Harris (1861–1931) came to Mahone Bay in 1884 to serve as curate or assistant to Rev. William Snyder. When Snyder died in October 1889, Harris became rector and remained at St. James for the rest of his life. In 1890 he married Florence Jane Zwicker (1859–1954), the daughter of Alfred and Louisa Zwicker and sister of A. C. "Monte" Zwicker.

Over the years Harris became a figure of great significance in the town. Writing in 1925, Clara Dennis described him as "a cultured man of the highest type." His importance extended far beyond his work as pastor of the Anglican church. "Throughout the county he is both reverenced and beloved. His home is open to all and a call there is an intellectual as well as a social treat. Indeed it is hard to measure the value of such a home to a community." As well, Harris "has taken a great interest in all public movements. He was the Father of the movement for the erection of the War Memorial which is such a credit to the town. And the monument was designed by him. He is also an enthusiastic Mason and takes much pride in their beautiful lodge room. Canon Harris is a leading authority on the history of the County and takes interest in the preservation of its historic spots." It was all true, and when he died in November 1931, he had served his congregation and community for an astonishing forty-seven years.

St. James Episcopal Church, Mahone, N. S.

St. James, c.1888   By the 1880s, St. James was again too small and was in poor condition, so the congregation decided to build a new larger church. Ned Harris feared that the Presbyterians, who had recently moved their church to the bottom of the hill closer to town, were hoping to "cut off Anglican stragglers." One cannot help suspecting that a more important reason for the move was to eliminate the need to climb the hill, especially in bad weather. Harris himself described on more than one occasion the difficulty of "getting up and down that fearful hill" when freezing rain made it icy.

For whatever reasons, Harris determined that "I am going to give all my energy to spur them into building the new [church] which has been in their mouths for years." Despite Snyder's grave reservations about the project, which caused a serious rift between the two men and divisions within the congregation, Harris triumphed. As the older man and senior minister, Snyder clearly was offended by Harris's enthusiastic, even aggressive, attitude, but to be fair, Snyder's concerns about the cost of the new church were partly justified. Harris initiated the project claiming that it would cost $5,100, whereas Snyder feared that it would cost about $8,000. Snyder proved to be right, although $7,000 had been raised by the time the church opened on September 27, 1887. As Harris quickly recognized, the congregation "are great people for coming out with the coins when they feel good, and they feel good when they have a lively sermon launched at them." He, of course, was a livelier preacher than Snyder. The old church was sold at public auction in July 1888 to Alfred F. Zwicker, for $40, on condition that he remove it within two months, which he did.

Construction of the new church was supervised by John E. Inglis, a member of the congregation, and members of the congregation provided much volunteer labour. All the interior finish was of native ash and other hardwoods—mahogany, maple, walnut, cherry, and oak—with pine used in the pews, and spruce in the roof and the panelling in the sanctuary, where it was backed with hardwood and glued tightly together. This was designed to intensify the sound produced in the chancel in the same way that the front and back of a violin intensify the sound produced by the reverberating strings of the instrument. Echo, on the other hand, was undesirable and was counteracted by cross-joists placed eighteen inches apart all over the roof and deeply recessed window jambs in the west wall of the building.

All the interior woodwork was given a rich natural finish, and carefully selected colours were applied to the plasterwork: blue on the chancel arch and on the hood moulds over the arch and the east window, gray on the capitals, rose on the clustered shafts of the pillars at the chancel entrance, and soft green on the walls. It was a rich and restful scheme, and it has been preserved by the congregation over the years. The exterior of the building was originally painted grey, but for more than fifty years now it has been a dusky yellow with brown and red trim, "a cheerful scheme" in the view of Rev. Robert Tuck, Ned Harris's grandson, "which suits the building well."

The steeple is thirty metres high and was shown on marine charts for many years as a guide to mariners. It used to be said that when approaching the harbour they could line up the spires of the three churches and be assured of being in a deep safe channel. The bell was cast in 1879 at the foundry on Fairmont Street operated by John and Angus McLeod. It was moved from the old church, where it had replaced the original smaller bell, which had developed a crack.

The church was originally lighted by oil lamps and subsequently by carbon gas generated in the cellar and distributed to the various outlets through a system devised by Ned Harris. In 1900 electricity was installed in the church, rectory, and parish hall. The original organ was built by Casavant Frères of Ste-Hyacinthe, Quebec, and was pumped by hand from a small closet entered through the door by the pulpit. Harry Eisenhaur was the organist for thirty-four years. A major refurbishment of the steeple and tower was undertaken in 1994 to replace the aging shingles and restore the paint. On August 28 of that year, the church was designated a provincial heritage property.

The architect of the new St. James was Ned's brother, William Critchlow Harris. He had trained as an architect with David Stirling in Halifax and in the course of his career designed many churches, typically in the High Victorian Gothic Revival style, blending elements of English and French Gothic. St. James epitomizes his mature style, which included broadly sloping roofs over large naves and smaller chancels, with Tudor arches everywhere, in nave and chancel windows and doorways. The buttressed exteriors were sheathed in board and batten cladding, and the steeples were made of three-stage towers defined by buttresses and dog-tooth ornament, surmounted by octagonal spires. The steeple of St. James was placed at the shoulder of the nave, where it is joined to the chancel, a position calculated to best catch the eye of the traveller entering or leaving the village by the shore road, which winds past the church and dominates the head of the bay.

Rev. Robert Tuck, a grandson of Ned and William Harris, describes St. James as "one of William Harris' loveliest creations…the crowning achievement of the early period of his career." Harris felt this himself, telling Ned that "if they keep to the plans you will have the best church in Nova Scotia!" In fact, St James is one of the few churches designed by Harris that was built exactly to his specifications. Inevitably, not everyone thought it beautiful, at least at first. One member of the congregation told Ned, admittedly before the building was completed, "that it might be all right inside, but outside it didn't look like a church at all, that he would take it for a factory!"

ST. JAMES RECTORY, 1907

Perhaps another reason why Harris was keen to build a new church at the bottom of the hill was that the rectory had been built there in 1847, on land purchased from John Mader for £30. Designed in the Gothic Revival style, the original house was a simple one-and-a-half storey building with three large, steeply-pitched gables on the front facade. Ned Harris described it in 1884 as "a nice cottage shaded by plenty of trees, with a lot of ground around it." By 1905 he wanted something more impressive, and undertook extensive modifications to the building, assisted by his architect brother. The roof was raised a full storey in height, and the building was redesigned in the Queen Anne Revival style. The remnants of the original roofline were left intact, however, and can still be seen on the interior of the attic end walls. It was claimed for many years that the house was haunted by the ghost of Snyder's first wife, Ann, who died there in 1878, although possibly she only haunted Ned Harris!

Happily, we have a description of the rectory as it appeared in the 1920s. According to Clara Dennis, "extending almost the length of one of the rooms is a brick fireplace with the unique cosey seat built inside, where one may sit and enjoy the comfort and warmth and observe the daily miracle of a tree turned into ash. But the attention is first attracted to the walls of the room on which are hung unusually fine paintings. They are the work of Canon Harris' brother, Robert Harris.… So the residents of Mahone do not have to go thousands of miles to see the work of this famous painter, but are more than favored in having this picture gallery in their midst." Robert Harris was a highly successful artist who is probably best known for his "Fathers of Confederation" painting, but he also made a number of fine sketches and paintings of Mahone Bay. This photo shows the rectory as it appeared after the renovations.

TRINITY UNITED CHURCH, C.1928

When the Methodist, Presbyterian, and Congregational churches of Canada joined together to form the United Church in 1925, Mahone Bay's Methodists moved over to the Presbyterian church, which was now named Trinity United. Curiously, the last minister at the Methodist church was Rev. Alban Daniel, who had been the first resident minister back in 1882 when he was still a probationer. When Trinity United's steeple was extensively damaged by a storm in 1928, the cost of replacing it was so high that a simple moulding was added instead. As a result, the church is distinctive from its two neighbours in not having a steeple. This photograph shows the church after the loss of the steeple.

KNOX PRESBYTERIAN CHURCH, 1926

When the United Church of Canada was formed in 1925, many Presbyterians throughout Canada refused to make the change. In Mahone Bay the dissidents built a new church, Knox Presbyterian, on the banks of the Anney River facing West Main and the war memorial in the centre of town. This was the former site of Anthony Langille's feed store. The land and church were a gift of prominent businessman T. G. Nicol, at a cost of $10,000. Rev. Robert Johnson preached the first sermon, but Rev. D. W. McDonald, a former missionary in Korea, was the first minister. The second marriage that took place in the church was that of Helen Nicol, daughter of T. G. Nicol, to Rev. D. W. McDonald.

A few years later the congregation built a hall over the river. This was used for various recreational activities until it was destroyed by fire. There were not enough Presbyterians to sustain Knox, however, and in 1961 it closed. The building reverted to the Nicol family, who later sold it to the Pentecostal church, which operates it as the Calvary Temple.

Chapter 7

Community Life

DOMINION DAY, C.1914

From the perspective of the early twenty-first century, it might seem that life in a small town in the nineteenth and early twentieth centuries must have been very dull. Such was not the case. Mahone Bay, like other small communities, enjoyed a very rich community life that included public events like celebrations and elections, recreational activities and the arts, involvement in social and fraternal societies, and of course the churches. There were also family events and sporting activities of all kinds.

People took their politics seriously then as now, and election campaigns often provided much entertainment and even excitement, especially in the era before the secret ballot was introduced. When Joseph Howe visited the area in April 1859, for example, Lunenburg merchant Adolphus Gaetz noted sourly that "the Arch Demagogue…has been perambulating the County…endeavouring to persuade ignorant people that their party are all right, and that their opponents are all wrong." And when the Reformers won that election and Howe became Premier, Gaetz claimed that it was because "one of the successful candidates flooded the place with Rum" and "bribery was practised to a fearful extent." As well, he claimed, the local Lutheran, Methodist, and Presbyterian clergy "preached daily and nightly political sermons" and "canvassed their people and urged upon them the necessity of voting for the Radicals." During the 1863 campaign, Charles Tupper, the Conservative leader, followed Howe through the county to "falsify many of the misstatements and infamous lies that Howe is spreading broad cast among the people." To Gaetz's great relief, the Conservatives won the election, both in Lunenburg County and provincially.

If political campaigns were boisterous and involved the distribution of rum in the 1850s, not much changed over the years, at least until recent times. C. U. Mader, the prominent merchant and shipowner, was also the leading Liberal in Mahone Bay for many years, and spared no effort in his party's cause. During the November 1909 provincial by-election won by A. K. MacLean, who was subsequently appointed attorney general, Mader was not above helping voters with their expenses if they would support his candidate. St. Clair Hiltz, a Lunenburger working in Halifax at the time, responded to Mader's letter "asking me to come out to vote for Hon. A. K. MacLean" that he would gladly do so if Mader paid his rail fare and two days' lost wages. "Say you send me a five [dollar bill] and a return ticket [and] i will be sure and come that is the best i can do Mr Mader for the party got pleanty money and i got none." This was not an isolated incident.

More recently, Ronald Crossland recalls his grandfather telling him that, because he "was voting one party and then there were others down the street, another party," when he had to go down to the post office on Main Street during election campaigns "you had to fight your way across the bridge." Dail Millett, who worked as a party organizer, recalls that on election day "you had to have a bottle of rum, a box of chocolates, and silk stockings" although in his opinion "it didn't help one bit" because people "would vote however they wanted. We had no way to tell but when the results came out we knew who had double-crossed us." Clearly, as Sir John A. Macdonald once observed, the introduction of the secret ballot in the 1870s encouraged a reprehensible degree of dishonesty among the voters!

Churches clearly played a very important role in community life, not only as places of worship but as the focal points for social activities. The churches were where baptisms, weddings, and funerals took place, and they organized many community activities as well. Happily, Ned Harris has left an extensive correspondence describing St. James's community activities, which, it can be assumed, were representative of what took place at the other churches as well.

Celebrations at religious holidays included children's concerts. At Easter 1884, for example, Harris attended a children's entertainment. "They have been practicing for it ever since I came, and I have been going to the practices, giving them a little bass. Of course, it was not very brilliant in my estimation, but to the people here it was a grand success. It was not bad at all for a country place. Mrs. Gray [wife of Dr. Charles Gray] had charge of it, and she was pretty glad to have it over, for it was a great deal of working training the youngsters."

Another local tradition associated with Easter was egg-tipping, a game in which people competed in knocking brightly painted hard-boiled eggs together tip to tip. The egg that cracked first had to be handed over to the owner of the stronger egg. At Easter 1884 Harris reported, "On Monday tip-egging was all the go here. They colour their eggs and go about the streets tipping. In the afternoon the Rector [William Snyder] filled his pockets and said, 'Come along to [Dr. Gray's house]. I want to tip eggs with my granddaughter.'"

Modern technology did not have a significant effect on Mahone Bay's community life until fairly recent years. In the 1940s Knaut's Hall was converted into a movie theatre, but it failed. It was succeeded by the Kenarick, which was housed in the former Knox church hall, but it was not successful either. Even so, there was an attempt in the 1950s to organize an annual film festival in the town, which also failed. While radio must have had some impact, the introduction of television undoubtedly has had the same baneful effect on community activities in Mahone Bay as elsewhere. Still, there are several local organizations that cater to those with particular interests, such as the garden club, bridge clubs, and the community garden. The recently established Mahone Bay Centre, which has taken over the old academy, is a focal point for community initiatives. Meanwhile, community events like the weekly flea markets during the summer months and the annual Wooden Boat Festival and Scarecrow Festival have made a difference in recent years as well.

SPION KOP HILL,
c.1910

One of the town's most popular sites was the hill—which is no longer there—at the top of Clairmont Street, where the tennis courts are now to be found. During the South African War (1899–1902), it was named Spion Kop, presumably to celebrate the battle fought on a hill of the same name near Ladysmith in January 1900. This is odd because the British lost that battle. In any event, an old cannon was acquired and placed at the top of the hill. People enjoyed walking up the hill and sitting on the cannon because of the fine view of the town and bay. The story is told that during the Second World War, Basil Eisenhauer got some wheels with the intention of including the cannon in a parade. When he went up the hill to put them on, the cannon was gone! Evan Burgoyne allegedly had sold it for scrap metal and given the money to the town. In this photograph, the mill pond can be seen in the background. It was later drained to create the town's water garden.

CORONATION DAY, 1937

Public celebrations were more popular in the past. New Year's Eve was tradition-ally celebrated by the firing of guns, a custom believed to bring good luck and drive away evil spirits. This tradition was brought from Germany and continues to this day in Mahone Bay and other Lunenburg County communities. Civic celebrations were also popular. In 1855, for example, December 27 was pro-claimed a "thanksgiving day" throughout the province by the lieutenant-gover-nor, "in consequence," as Adolphus Gaetz recorded in his diary, "of the success of the Allied Armies in the War with Russia, and also for the abundant Harvest yielded to our Farmers, & Fishermen throughout the Province."

Eight years later the marriage of the Prince of Wales was celebrated in April 1863 with parades that included the militia, clergy, magistrates, and Masons, and the firing of salutes and the ringing of church bells. Dominion Day was celebrat-ed after 1867, of course, and in later years Empire Day (May 24) as well. The coronation of King George VI in 1937 was a very special event, especially after the 1936 abdication crisis, which had abruptly ended the brief reign of Edward VIII. The coronation was celebrated in Mahone Bay, as elsewhere throughout the Commonwealth, with a parade and speeches. This photograph shows Mayor A. C. Zwicker addressing the crowd.

**IOOF PARADE,
c.1890**

Parades were always popular. This undated photograph shows a parade by the Independent Order of Foresters (IOOF) on South Main Street, led by the brass band. In the background can be seen (left to right) George Westhaver's oar and block factory, Titus Langille's shipyard shed, and his brother Alfred Langille's tin shop (flying the IOOF banner because the society's headquarters was upstairs). This building was later the home of D. A. Burgoyne's plumbing and heating business. Today it houses the Gazebo Café.

GOOD FRIDAY PARADE, 1909

One curious tradition in Mahone Bay was the annual parade on Good Friday. This photograph shows a crowd gathered on South Main Street waiting for it to start, as the town band is getting itself organized. This indicates that the photograph was taken sometime after 1884. W. H. S. Zwicker's store can be seen on the right and George Westhaver's fine home is in the centre background.

CITIZENS' DAY PARADE, C.1935   It is not known precisely what Citizens' Day was but it appears to have been an occasion for a holiday and parade during the summer months.

MAHONE BAY BAND, C.1914

Of course, parades and other civic events were greatly enhanced when brass bands were organized in the town. The best known was undoubtedly the Mahone Bay Brass Band, organized in 1884 and led for many years by W. E. Delaney and subsequently by Harry Eisenhauer, Snyder Slauenwhite, and Warren Hirtle. In the early 1890s it became attached to Annapolis County's 69th Militia Regiment, which, with Lunenburg County's 75th Regiment spent two weeks every summer at the Aldershot training camp near Kentville. The other town band was the Lutheran St. John Association band organized and trained by Rev. A. R. J. Graepp, who also later trained the Bach Amateur Orchestra at Bridgewater.

This photograph was probably taken at the annual Aldershot training camp just before the outbreak of the First World War. Harry Eisenhauer is seated on the left side. The man standing on the far right with the bass horn is Snyder Slauenwhite. After the First World War the band became a civilian unit and carried on until the late 1940s. It practised in the old town hall and later used a room at the rear of the present town hall.

MASONIC GATHERING, 1890s

Mahone Bay had numerous fraternal organizations, such as the Masonic Lodge, the IOOF, and the Orange Order, as well as the Women's Institute, and Scouts and Brownies for the children. The Charity Lodge of the Masonic Order was founded at Mahone Bay in 1874. It held its organizational meeting at Knaut's Hall, and Lewis Knaut was the first Worshipful Master. It soon became a significant organization in the community and in 1918 purchased the building that had housed Allan Strum's oil clothes factory and converted it into a Masonic lodge. Ned Harris designed the lodge and supervised its construction and even carved the woodwork and painted the scenes. Clara Dennis described it in 1925 as "an artistic gem." This photograph shows a gathering of Masons in front of the Anglican rectory. Although undated, it was taken before the 1905 renovations to the rectory.

CHRISTMAS, 1915   The tradition of having a Christmas tree in the house originated in Germany and was brought to England by Prince Albert, Queen Victoria's husband. It soon spread throughout the empire. Here we have a very early photograph of a Christmas tree in the home of Harriet Bruhm on Fairmont Street. Harriet's daughter, Louise, is also shown. It seems appropriate that Lunenburg County has since become the centre of the Christmas tree industry in eastern Canada.

BOATING, C.1910   Inevitably, the scenic bay encouraged boating activities, and picnics on its beaches and islands were also popular. One especially festive outing occurred in August 1886, when the tug *Ralph E. S.* sailed from Mahone Bay to Chester Basin carrying several passengers and the town band. According to the *Lunenburg Progress-Enterprise,* "quite a number of American visitors were there and all hands seemed to enjoy themselves immensely. At about 8 pm a violinist appeared on the scene and the light fantastic was tripped by lovers of dancing, until the witching hour of midnight approached, when all retired to their respective homes in their respective conveyances very much pleased with the day's pleasure and loud in their praises of Mr. Mills," who had paid for it all. This photograph shows two well-dressed women about to climb into a dory for an outing. Ambrose Eisenhaur's carriage factory is in the background.

Jigging for cod, c.1910

Jigging for cod was and remains a popular pastime, especially at Oakland. This photograph shows Ethel Hirtle (right) with two unidentified friends, jigging for cod.

Ladies outing, c.1910

These well-dressed ladies, one of whom seems to have brought along her son, appear to be enjoying an outing. Their carriage can be seen behind them, and the shop in the background indicates that they are on South Main Street.

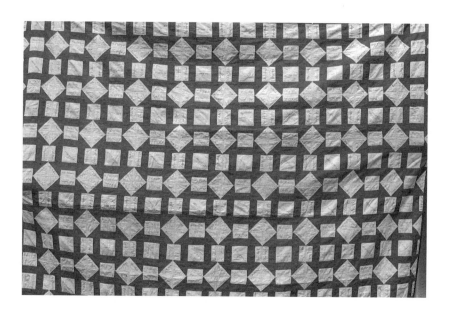

SIGNATURE QUILT,
c.1880

Churches have always engaged in fund-raising activities, and, of course, it is essential to make them enjoyable in order to get people involved. Garden parties were popular well into the twentieth century. Dennis Zwicker recalls that "the biggest event" for children in the 1930s was the garden party. All churches but the Lutheran held garden parties, but the Anglican party was the biggest and best, which Zwicker rightly attributed to Ned Harris. "He had great ideas. The whole grounds, they would stretch wires and they would hang lanterns with different colour paper on them."

At one church sale, held in the 1880s to help pay for the new Anglican church, Harris "tried an election." It was a sort of popularity contest, but those wishing to vote had to pay a poll tax. "It worked pretty well, though it took a good while to get it into their intellects what was going on," he reported. "However, when the little girls and boys grasped the notion they canvassed the men in style. I had a great laugh at the result though—I went in with a large majority, and was cheered accordingly. Dr. Gray was going to contest the election, declaring I had bribed [the electorate], inasmuch as he had seen me give four or five boys the amount of the poll tax to go and vote."

Another church fundraising project was the so-called signature quilt. This involved soliciting contributions from members of the congregation, in return for which they signed their names on a square of material that was then sewn into the quilt. Very few Nova Scotian signature quilts have survived, but the Settlers Museum has a magnificent one, recently donated by Trinity United Church, which dates back to the 1880s. The signatures of various citizens of the village can still be clearly read, making the quilt a priceless tangible connection to the community 125 years ago.

CARRIAGE RIDE, c.1910
Here we see Ambrose Eisenhaur taking his granddaughter for a ride in one of his own carriages.

SLEDDING, c.1890
These men appear to be enjoying an old-fashioned sleigh ride. Note the man in the centre of the photograph who has brought out a chair to get into the picture.

MAHONE BAY HOCKEY TEAM, c.1910

They didn't have modern equipment and they played on the mill pond or on the harbour, but Mahone Bay boys enjoyed hockey as much as boys elsewhere in Canada. This photograph shows the high school team about 1910. Left to right (back): Aubrey Joudrey, Chester Millett, Bruce Archibald, Spurgeon Hirtle, Edward Harris, Morris Maxner; (seated) Harold Joudrey, Basel Cushing, Gordon Daury.

ICE FISHING, 1942   Ice fishing has always been popular, and with luck it also puts fresh fish on the table. This photograph shows men jigging for smelts in January 1942. There couldn't have been a lot of snow that year, as one man has actually brought his bicycle.

10665 Mahone. N. S. from H. & S. W. Railway.

EXHIBITION BUILDING, 1900

In 1885 an exhibition building was constructed on Clearway Street facing West Main. The first Lunenburg County Exhibition was held there in 1886, and a few more exhibitions were held there in subsequent years. They were not a success financially, however, and were discontinued. The building was later used for several years for bazaars, fairs, and parties, and for skating carnivals in winter. People wore fanciful costumes to these carnivals, allegedly following the example of the Marquis of Lorne, Canada's governor general from 1878 to 1883, who organized carnivals on Ottawa's canals. The building gradually fell into disuse, however, and was sold in 1919 to Ambrose Eisenhaur, who demolished it a year later. The exhibition building is the domed structure at the right side of this photograph, which was taken in 1900.

"The Mamie Bay Exhibition Bld, circa 1884" Graham Baker — 1979 for Mr. & Mrs. Hyson

TIMOTHY LANTZ'S GIANT PUMPKIN, 1887

This fine painting of the exhibition building was done by Graham Baker for Herbie Hyson in 1979, and is now proudly owned by Andrew Whynot. It portrays Timothy Lantz of Clearland, whose giant pumpkin won first prize at the 1887 exhibition. The pumpkin went on to the Grand Colonial Exhibition in London, where Mr. Lantz received a scroll and medal from Queen Victoria.

MAKING MUSIC, c.1910

There has always been music in Mahone Bay, of course. Obed Ham, the shipbuilder, wrote music as well as poetry, and not only played the violin but made instruments as well. Simeon Jodrey also made violins in a little workshop behind his home, the old William Begin house, on West Main. There were also amateur theatrical societies that performed plays and revues from time to time.

In the 1930s Trixie Hay-Campbell operated the Mayfair Studio on Pleasant Street, which offered classes in drama and perhaps dance. At the end of December 1937 a revue was "colourfully and charmingly presented" at Knox Hall "before large and interested audiences," according to the *South Shore Record,* "under the auspices of the Mahone Bay Fire Department." The Women's Institute also organized concerts such as the one held in December 1933 that included solos, dialogues, readings, a play, a folk dance, and a "drill" entitled "Two little pickaninnies," which was "comical to say the least," in the words of the *South Shore Record.* Dance music was provided through the 1930s by the popular Melody Makers.

The Hirtle family was active in musical circles. This photograph shows (left to right) Emma Hirtle and her sister Ethel, who was a popular soloist at the Baptist church, and their friend Mabel Hardy. Emma and Ethel Hirtle were sisters of Warren Hirtle, who was himself an active musician and headed the Mahone Bay brass band for many years.

**ALICE HAGEN
IN HER STUDIO,
C.1960**

Born in Halifax, Alice Hagen (1872–1972) attended the Nova Scotia College of Art and Design, then called the Victoria School of Art and Design, and also studied with Adelaide Alsop Robineau in New York. She opened her own studio in Halifax in 1898. After marrying John Hagen, an official with the British Cable Company, she spent several years in Jamaica. They retired to Mahone Bay in 1932, and Alice lived for the last forty years of her life on Clairmont Street, where she made pottery and taught many students.

According to the program for a 1984 retrospective showing of her work at the Anna Leonowens Gallery in Halifax, Alice Hagen, using local materials and establishing her own techniques, developed "a ware using mingled coloured clays of blue, white and green, which she called Scotian Pebble." She achieved an international reputation, and her work can be seen at the Settlers Museum, the DesBrisay Museum, the Nova Scotia Museum, and the Mount Saint Vincent University Art Gallery. A building at the Nova Scotia College of Art and Design has been named in her honour.

ALICE HAGEN CHINA AND POTTERY   Alice Hagen originally specialized in china painting, which was very popular in the late nineteenth century as part of the Arts and Crafts Movement, but in later years she taught herself how to make pottery as well. She also painted. This photograph shows a display of lustre and glass pieces painted by Alice Hagen, including (centre, top shelf) a vase with a portrait of the Mik'maq artist Christianna Morris, as displayed at the Settlers Museum in Mahone Bay. The vases on the bottom shelf are decorated with patterns taken from Maxfield Parrish paintings, which Alice Hagen much admired.

Recommended Reading

Anonymous. *South Shore: Seasoned Timbers. Some Historic Buildings from Nova Scotia's South Shore.* Vol. 2. Halifax: Heritage Trust of Nova Scotia, 1974.

Balcom, B. A. *History of the Lunenburg Fishing Industry.* Lunenburg: Lunenburg Marine Museum Society, 1977.

Bell, Winthrop Pickard. *The "Foreign Protestants" and the Settlement of Nova Scotia.* Toronto: University of Toronto Press, 1961.

Bellerose, George. *Facing the Open Sea: The People of Big Tancook Island.* Halifax: Nimbus, 1995.

Corkum, Hugh H. *On Both Sides of the Law.* Hantsport: Lancelot, 1989.

Crooker, William S. *Oak Island Gold.* Halifax: Nimbus, 1993.

DesBrisay, Mather Byles. *History of the County of Lunenburg.* Toronto: William Briggs, 1895.

Fergusson, C. Bruce, ed. *The Diary of Adolphus Gaetz.* Halifax: Public Archives of Nova Scotia, 1965.

Foran, Joan, et al. *Dear Old Mahone: Historic Images of Mahone Bay, Nova Scotia, and Surrounding Communities.* Mahone Bay: Settlers Museum, 2004.

Franklin, Paul. "A heritage of craftsmanship." *Wooden Boat* (September/October 1998), 39-42. (Profile of Cecil Heisler.)

Hatt, Herbert. *Alive to All True Values: My Ninety Years' Experience.* Hantsport: Lancelot, 1988.

Huber, Paul B., and Eva Maria, eds. *European Origins and Colonial Travails: The Settlement of Lunenburg.* Halifax: Messenger Publications, 2003.

Irwin, E. H. Rip. *A Complete Guide to Lighthouses and Lights of Nova Scotia.* Halifax: Nimbus, 2003.

Lacey, Laurie, ed. *Lunenburg County Folklore and Oral History: Project '77.* Ottawa: National Museums of Canada, 1979.

Mahone Bay Pioneers. *A Forgotten Industry: A Short History of Shipbuilding in Mahone Bay.* Mahone Bay: Settlers Museum, 1996.

Mitcham, Allison. *Offshore Islands of Nova Scotia and New Brunswick.* Hantsport: Lancelot, 1984.

Morrison, James H., and James Moreira, eds. *Tempered by Rum: Rum in the History of the Maritime Provinces.* Porters Lake: Pottersfield Press, 1988.

Parker, Mike. *Historic Lunenburg.* Halifax: Nimbus, 1999.

Robertson, Barbara R. *Sawpower: Making Lumber in the Sawmills of Nova Scotia.* Halifax: Nimbus/Nova Scotia Museum, 1986.

Robinson, Geoff & Dorothy. *Duty-Free.* Summerside: privately published, 1992.

———. *It Came by the Boat Load.* Summerside: privately published, 1989.

Tuck, Robert C. *Letters from Mahone Bay.* Charlottetown: Maplewood Books, 2001.

———. *Gothic Dreams: The Life and Times of a Canadian Architect William Critchlow Harris 1854–1913.* Toronto: Dundurn, 1978.

Yeadon, Marina Cavanaugh. *The Early Dwellings of Mahone Bay, Nova Scotia, 1754–1850: A Preliminary Guide to the Early Domestic Architecture of Mahone Bay and Area.* Mahone Bay: Settlers Museum, 1995.

Photo Credits

The images used in this book are courtesy of the following individuals and institutions. References are to the pages on which they appear.

Fisheries Museum of the Atlantic. 33, 41, 43, 50, 59, 69, 131.

Hennigar, David. 11, 18, 20, 32, 35, 39, 44b, 45t, 54, 56, 91, 92, 94, 97, 106, 111t, 113, 119t, 120, 130, 133, 137, 154.

Lunenburg County Historical Society, Fort Point Museum Collection. 122, 123, 143.

Mahone Bay Settlers Museum. 4, 16, 17, 21, 37, 40, 42, 45b, 46, 47t, 48, 51, 52, 53, 61, 62, 66, 70, 71, 72b, 73, 77, 82, 89, 90, 93b, 102, 104, 107, 108, 109, 110, 112, 115, 116, 117, 118, 121, 124, 127, 132, 133, 140, 141, 146, 147, 148, 149, 150, 152, 153, 155b, 156, 157, 164.

Maritime Museum of the Atlantic. 25, 60, 63, 67.

Nova Scotia Archives and Records Management. vi, 2, 6, 9, 10, 12, 14, 15, 26, 44t, 47b, 49, 55, 57, 58, 81, 99, 100, 103b, 159, 160.

Nova Scotia Museum. 22, 29, 30, 31, 73, 79.

Parks Canada Canadian Inventory of Historic Buildings. 78, 85, 87, 88, 105.

Anonymous, 23; Dalhousie University Library, William Inglis Morse Collection, 8; DesBrisay Museum, 83, 158; Betty Eisenhauer, 84; Harry Eisenhauer, 114; Joan Foran, 80, 86, 111b, 128, 151; Evelyn Hutt, 28; Carolyn Kuhn, 96, 101; Alex MacDonald, 142; Judith Mader, 155t, 162; Mount St Vincent University Art Gallery, 163; Wilma Stewart-White, 76; Brian Tennyson, 72t, 75, 93t, 126, Rev Robert Tuck, 38, 134, 136, 139; Andrew Whynot, 161; Peter Young, 95; Terry Young, 27.

Index

Martin's River 94.
Mason, David 26.
Mason, Leslie 26.
Mason, Stan 26.
Mason's Island 24.
Masonic Order 152.
Mauger, Joshua 7, 77, 124, 126.
Maxner, Morris 158.
Mayfair Studio 162.
McDonald, Donald 102.
McDonald, Rev. D.W. 142.
McDonald, Ronald 8, 73, 88, 120.
McDougald, A.J. 22.
McInnis, Daniel 29.
McInnis Jr, Daniel 29.
McKay, Donald 44.
McKinnon, John 127.
McLean, Catherine 82.
McLean, Charles 46, 60, 82.
McLean, Ella 82.
McLean, John 13, 44, 45, 46, 82.
McLean, Lenora Agnes 82.
McLean, William 46, 60, 82.
McLean shipyard 19, 44, 45, 46, 50, 51,
    54, 56, 66, 68, 69; fire 60.
McLeod, John & Angus 138.
McLeod, Robert 98.
McMullen, John 29.
McNab, Rev. Ebenezer 127, 128.
McVay, George 89.
McVay yacht-building company 89.
Merchant, Eric & Vida 86.
Methodist church. See Churches.
Mi'kmaq 1, 2, 5, 10-11, 24.
Militia 99, 151.
Millbury, Seth 80.
Miller, Eric 84.
Millett, Chester 158.
Millett, Dail 111, 144.
Millett, Freeman 119.
Millett, James B. 118, 119.
Mitchell, George 114.
Moody, Rev. T.T. 125.
Moorsom, William 10.
Morals 19.
Moreau, Rev. J.B. 7.
Morris, Christianna 164.
Morton, Rev. R.S. 133.
Mosher, Fred 42.
Mushamush River 1, 5, 11, 100.
Music 48, 162.

Naas, Captain George 34.

Nelson, William 29.
New Year's Eve 147.
Nicol, Helen 142
Nicol, T.G. 17, 142.
Northwest Cove (Tancook Island) 25.
Northwest Range 133.
Nova Scotia Yacht and Boatbuilders Ltd
    62.
Nureyev, Rudolf 108.
Nursing homes 102.

Oak Island. 1, 29, 30.
Oakland 44, 75, 155.
Oakland power station 16-17.
Old Settlers' Place Restaurant 77.
Olive & Taylor Pharmacy 96, 113.
Olive, Dr. Allan 113.
Orange Order 152.
Orth, George 132.
Oxen 12, 35, 51, 111, 135. 157.

Parades. Citizens' Day 150; Good Friday
    149; IOOF 148.
Pearl, Albert 33.
Pearl, Benjamin 33.
Pearl, Walter 33.
Pearl, Warren 26.
Pearl Island 33.
Peggy's Cove 26.
Penney family 118.
Pernette, Joseph 4, 7, 77.
Petite Rivière 36.
Pickels, Ann 72.
Pickels, Dr. George , 43, 72, 113.
Pirates 1, 29, 30.
Plum Island 30.
Pool Halls 19.
Pooley, Henry 74, 99.
Population 15, 17.
Port Hawkesbury 60.
Post office 21, 122, 144.
Presbyterian church. See Churches.
Privateers 7.
Prohibition 18-20, 54, 63-5.

Quaker Island 24.
Queen Charlotte Island. See Tancook
    Island
Quilting 156.
Quinlan, Clara 107, 108.
Quinlan, John 107.

Race track 20.

Images of our Past

Uncovering the rich history of the Maritimes, one community at a time.
Check out these and other *Images of Our Past* titles at your local bookstore
or online at www.nimbus.ns.ca

Historic Pictou

Historic Guysborough

Historic Dartmouth

Historic North End Halifax

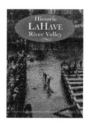

Historic LaHave River Valley

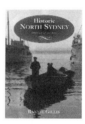

Historic North Sydney

Historic Lunenburg

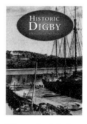

Historic Digby

Historic Colchester